Maury
Wednesday's
Child

Maury
Wednesday's Child

Maury Blair with **Doug Brendel**

BETHANY HOUSE PUBLISHERS
MINNEAPOLIS, MINNESOTA 55438
A Division of Bethany Fellowship, Inc.

The events in this book are true; only the names of a few individuals have been changed, in order to protect their privacy, or to avoid any possible embarrassment.

Originally published in Canada by
Mainroads Productions, Inc.
under the title, *Child of Woe*

Maury, Wednesday's Child
Maury Blair, with Doug Brendel

Library of Congress Catalog Card Number 82-072580

ISBN 0-87123-323-1

Published by Bethany House Publishers
A Division of Bethany Fellowship, Inc.
6820 Auto Club Road, Minneapolis, Minnesota 55438

Printed in the United States of America

Dedicated
to my wife, Bev,
given to me by God as a gift,
a vessel of healing
and encouragement.
Her support has been vital,
not only in the mission that
this book represents
but in the full scope of my life.

And
to our daughters,
Lisa and Laury,
more precious treasures than
this child of woe could have ever imagined.

ACKNOWLEDGMENTS

Heartfelt thanks to two very special people in particular among the many who have helped me in the preparation of this book.

My close friend Eddie Brunet provided great encouragement for the effort and paved the way for the project with much practical advice and support.

Anne Barry, my assistant at Toronto Teen Challenge, is an important part of our ministry. Anne was instrumental in drawing the story out of me, which cleared the first hurdle for the book to be written. She also accomplished the huge task of transcribing hours of interviews with Doug Brendel, which cleared the final hurdle for the book to be written.

FOREWORD

How we hold the blade determines the depth and hurt of the cut. This truth echoes man's responsibility in how he handles the bludgeonings of life. As Shakespeare noted:

Men at some times are masters of their fates;
The fault, dear Brutus, is not in our stars,
But in ourselves.

Maury Blair, the director of Toronto Teen Challenge and Break-Through Ministries, is living truth of this premise. While some, who are brutalized by those with power over them, succumb to bitterness, anger, and resentment, Maury has not. He is better, not bitter.

Maury, Wednesday's Child frankly tells of times of terror and senseless emotional and physical brutality. The pain is there as you trace Maury's tragedy through the tears. We can identify in a small way with his horror because all of us have felt at some time the pang of rejection, feeling unwanted. As Romeo said, "He jests at scars that never felt a wound."

Maury is a surprise. He is my friend. He has spoken in my church. He is so well adjusted that no one could suspect today that he was predisposed to violence and disaster in childhood. Like his Bible counterpart, Jabez (1 Chronicles 4:9, 10), Maury became the joy of his family.

How all this happened is one of life's most remarkable stories. *Maury, Wednesday's Child* verbalizes the unspeakable, exposes emotions of rage and anger, and then points clearly to the only One who can "Rescue the Perishing." You must read it. *Maury, Wednesday's Child* offers promise for the emotionally damaged.

Ron Hembree
Evangelist and Author

ABOUT THE WRITER

DOUG BRENDEL, a young Christian freelance writer, spent hundreds of hours with Maury and his family to capture the story of *Maury, Wednesday's Child*. Doug has written several books, including the Nita Edwards story, *Miracle in the Mirror*, and other materials behind the scenes for a variety of Christian organizations and personalities, including Pat Robertson, Rex Humbard, James Robison, and the Full Gospel Business Men's Fellowship International. His wife, Cathy, has taught special education in public schools for seven years and they make their home in the Chicago area.

CONTENTS

Introduction

O Memory! thou fond deceiver.
Oliver Goldsmith, 1764

INTRODUCTION

When Maury Blair walks into a room, he lights it up. He is a source of joy and fun and warmth everywhere he goes. Hard to grasp, then, the fact that this gregarious man of God is the same Maury Blair who survived for years as a refugee in his own home, a victim of the horrors of child abuse and revenge.

As Maury and Bev and I worked our way through the terrible tale, discussing the sordid details hour after hour, I had to notice the remarkable lack of malice that Maury displayed. Even those characters who had done him the most harm were described with care and consideration. I found myself flinching angrily as I heard about many of the people who populated his past, people I regarded as selfish or irresponsible or even criminal in their behaviour. But Maury steadfastly clung to a loving and hopeful view.

Throughout the project I pressured Maury to tell the story with no holds barred, with all the ugliness exposed. Maury, on the other hand, always seemed to hold back, and as the writer looking for the most dramatic story possible, I was frustrated. It was not until the final rendering of the manuscript, after days of writing and rewriting in conference with Maury and Bev, that I realized what had happened.

Maury's personal revolution — the inner working of the Heavenly Father in his life — had completely transformed him, all the way down to his memory. As a child of the King, Maury now sees his past through eyes of love. Each villain is now perceived as a victim, each vicious act as the sad outgrowth of sin. While the outsider's reaction might be one of fury, Maury can only feel compassion for those who wronged him. Like the martyr Stephen, so pure in death, Maury wants no sins laid to their charge.

Moreover, Maury insisted on protecting those he loved the most — his family, his brothers and sisters, his friends — from hurt. Maury researched his own background extensively, and may know more details about his family's heritage than any of his relatives. Many parts of the story were written, then shrunken, then finally expunged altogether as Maury agonized over the effect their publication would have on his loved ones.

It gripped me to see this: a man driven in his spirit to tell his sad story, compelled by God and by dozens of friends and advisers across North America to expose the truth for the good of so many thousands of others who will be touched and helped by it — and yet a man constrained by love to sacrifice powerful elements of the story for the sake of his brothers and sisters and their families. Many times during the project I challenged Maury on the subject, but his priorities were rock-solid. There is much to admire in the man Maury Blair, but as I pulled the final page out of the typewriter, I felt the keenest admiration for this quality in him.

Many names, then, as well as places and dates, have been altered. Some segments of the chronology have been omitted or bridged over. But in all other respects the story you are about to read is true. The grotesque nature of some scenes is by no means exaggerated; if anything, Maury has insisted that the nastiest extremes be toned down.

From the beginning, Maury has also insisted that his story is worth nothing if it bears no fruit, if it has no ministry in the life of the reader. His prayer, as he turns himself inside out and exposes the very beating of his heart, is that this book will express the love of the Heavenly Father.

Yes, it is a gruesome story. It is horrible in places. And yet, ultimately, it is a story charged through and through with the beauty and majesty of the grace of a loving Heavenly Father. Against a backdrop of human cruelty and suffering, it is a story of God's boundless love and mercy.

Doug Brendel
Chicago

CHAPTER ONE
The Animal's Prey

The Lord hath called me from the womb;
from the bowels of my mother hath
he made mention of my name.

— *Isaiah 49:1*

CHAPTER ONE
The Animal's Prey

The child was gaunt, half from poverty, half from nerves, hollow around the eyes, his triangular face drawn down into a grim, empty expresssion that did not even qualify as a frown. His hair, straight and dark and thin, was poorly cut and not very clean, and it ran all over his head at will. His skin, which should have been rosy pink at the age of seven, was a deathly yellowish gray.

He would stand in a far corner of the bedroom, the dark corner, away from the door, staring out the window onto the yard and beyond to the bridge where the train tracks disappeared. He had perfected his technique, night after night, of standing so motionless that he could attract no undue attention. There was no place to hide in the house; but here, in the solemn darkness of the lonely bedroom, he could at least place four or five feet of distance between himself and the landing at the top of the stairs. But the fear was too much to face. The child would always face the window, his back to the door.

The house was an old stucco, loose enough of construction that everyone in it could tell where everyone else was. The brothers and sisters could be playing and chatting and arguing on the lower level, with Mother in the kitchen, and the solitary child upstairs could hear it all. When the danger was not so very present, he often slipped to the floor of the landing, lying flat on his skinny belly, with his chin resting on his knuckles, peering through the grating of the floor vent to the activity below. With the lights out upstairs, this vent and the bedroom window provided the only narrow shafts of light in the child's world.

He gravitated to the light coming out of the floor as if it were a familiar friend, the kind one grows up playing stickball with in the streets. Except that the child had no such friends.

And then the old loose house would tell its inhabitants that someone else had arrived. Invariably the children downstairs would settle into an uneasy quiet as the old man lifted himself, drunken, up the steps of the cement porch, then lumbered to the screen door, which squealed when you opened it and hissed and slapped at you when you let it go behind you.

So the old man was home again. He could be heard roaring and then grumbling and then roaring again, cursing profusely in his drunken stupor, growling as he stumbled around the lower level. The children and the mother made room for him, much as one willingly gets out of the way of a big, unfriendly animal. But none of these people were the animal's prey.

Upstairs, the telltale slapping of the screen door sent a silent scream of alarm through the child. He jumped up in a single reflexive motion from his cozy place by the light on the floor and slipped through the bedroom door and far back into the corner to the window. He had learned to move quickly, before the old man could hear him leaving the vent. He had learned not to hide under the covers. He had learned not to hide at all. It was useless. Only standing straight and silent in the black corner of the room, looking motionless out the window, could he sometimes avoid the horror.

And finally, after a minute or an hour of growling and snarling obscenities, the old man headed for the staircase. As each stair bent under his weight, the child suppressed a shiver. He tried not to tremble, because trembling could trigger the monster.

The old man could take two routes. Each night it was a question of which he would choose. As he drew himself up the top step, he could either turn to his left, toward the bathroom and his bedroom, or he could keep coming, straight ahead, through the door of the child's room. The child could always feel him mounting the top step. The boy waited in the shadows and prayed desperately, silently, that the old man would make the turn, make the turn, make the turn.

Sometimes, if he had taken in too little liquor to exhaust himself, the old man could think clearly enough to sense the child's anguish; and then he relished that moment when he came to the landing at the top of the stairs...relished making the child squirm inwardly while the decision was waiting to be made.

To the frail and narrow child, he was a huge man, although he was of no more than normal build, distinguished only by a bald head and a mustache. But his strong hands were punctuated by powerful, stout fingers. Standing on the landing, staring into the bedroom at the child's slender silhouette, the old man looked like a volcanic mountain, longing to explode, but unconvinced of the value of expending the energy.

And he stood cursing, all the time cursing, on the landing. From the moment he began his long climb up the stairs, the ugly poison could be heard pouring forth all through the house. Depending on the extent of his drunkenness, he would rage like a bull or mutter like a threatened dog, but always as he approached the head of the stairs his words were the same, fixed on the pale skinny child, his face a splash of white by the window in the far corner:

"You black b————...I'm gonna kill you, you black b————."

The very words drew the child's muscles tight, strung up by unrelieved panic. And then, when the worst would be realized, the old man would fail to make the turn, and his drunken steps would carry him through the bedroom door and toward the terrified boy.

"You black b————...I'm gonna kill you."

The child could feel the heat of his body as he approached. He could smell the liquor. He could almost taste the rage.

The old man seized him by the upper arm, his great fingers wrapping around the child's limb as if it were a broomhandle. With his other hand he pushed the boy against the wall, then drew back his hand and closed his fingers into a colossal fist.

For the rest of the family, it was an exercise in helplessness. The mother always tried in vain to stop the old man before he ever got to the steps. But he always managed to shout her down or — more often — wait out the confrontation and slip around her to the stairway. Then, as the children downstairs jumped in surprise to the sound of the child's body hitting the wall upstairs, the beleaguered mother bolted for the stairway. Downstairs, the children, at the various ages, had not all learned to ignore the horrible episodes. The older ones looked awkwardly at each other, or at the floor. The younger ones looked wildly from face to face, seeking the relief of explanation, looking for someone to stop the shrieking from upstairs.

The old man punched the child until he grew bored, then threw the boy on the floor like a rag doll and began kicking him. The child cried out until the cries choked in his throat; then he just struggled to keep breathing. With the horror of the scene pressing in on him, the boy could still remember clearly not to resist more than he had to; resisting, he always remembered, made the old man crazier.

And finally, with the rage released, the old man came to rest. Still muttering about the "black bastard," he turned and lurched around the corner, into the bathroom, where he would relieve himself of some of his liquor — if he could stand up long enough.

The child lay in a heap, gasping and crying quietly, his body pounding with pain, his mind spinning furiously with questions.

Why does he hate me? Why is this happening to me? Why doesn't anyone want me?

Long after the old man had tramped out of the bathroom and dumped himself in bed, the child could risk picking himself up off the cold wooden floor. Sometimes one of his brothers would be there to help him up, to check over his bruises and make sure nothing was broken.

And sometimes, when the child failed to get up, the brothers would tap him and call his name: "Maury...Maury ...Are you all right?"

It was strange, in a way, to hear that question in connection with my own name. There was nothing right about me. I was the despised black bastard, and I didn't know why.

CHAPTER TWO
Side-Tracked

When lovely woman stoops to folly,
And finds too late that men betray,
What charm can soothe her melancholy?
What art can wash her guilt away?

— *Oliver Goldsmith, 1766*

CHAPTER TWO
Side-Tracked

Of all the Peters sisters, and there were seven of them besides the two brothers, Alice Peters showed the most promise. Her mother was a fat stern woman who took her Christianity very, very seriously, thank you — and she was thrilled when Alice packed off for Bible school in New Jersey.

It was a long way from the Peters home in Paris, Ontario, and Alice was a little intimidated being so far away and bearing the responsibility of performance. She kept mostly to herself on campus, and her grades were reasonably good.

And as she studied more and more of the Scriptures, she felt within her a restless calling to the evangelistic field.

Her friends delightedly nicknamed her Aimee as she took to the preaching circuit. The preaching ministry of Aimee Semple McPherson was at its zenith of popularity, and they swore that Alice would follow in her anointed footsteps. Churches found that Alice was a good preacher. Her meetings were successful, and they grew generally larger from season to season as she criss-crossed the North American continent with her simple gospel message.

There were drawbacks, however, to being Mother's favourite. When Mrs. Peters took sick, she wanted no one else to care for her. Her enthusiasm for Alice's ministry stopped when her own well-being came into question. The other sisters were less inclined to lend a hand to the cross old woman anyway. So Alice reluctantly left her ministry — only for a little while, she decided — to stay at home with her ailing mother.

At least this is the story we heard later.

There was little money to spend. The Peters family had

never been wealthy. Alice searched out a job in Paris and settled into the nurse's routine. Her mother was crabby or pitiful, depending on her mood, and it grated on Alice. It was hard to maintain a proper, positive Christ-like outlook on life with this burden whining at her all the time.

Mother's old car was making a funny sound one day, and Alice took it to a repair shop. The motor mechanic looked both at the car and at Alice. She, in turn found him attractive, in a coarse way, smeared with axle grease and motor oil and dirt, shiny with perspiration.

His name was Bob Wick — a fun-loving socializer, the worldly-wise gentleman in every sense. He was accustomed to a little drinking with friends at the hotel bar at the end of the day. Reluctantly at first, Alice joined him.

But she grew accustomed to Bob's lifestyle as well. Somehow, in the weeks that followed, her spiritual perspective slipped out of focus.

Almost helplessly, she wandered into a new, sad life.

Tongues wagged all through the town. The townspeople loved good gossip, and this relationship — after Alice's work in the ministry — provided the best of fodder. Here was the beautiful side-tracked lady evangelist, in love with the handsome, rough-hewn mechanic.

There were evidences of goodness in the relationship, elements that Alice could hook into emotionally and use to rationalize away her shattered morality. Bob was courteous to her, a gentleman. He was faithful to her, making her his only object of affection. They doted on each other. It felt like Alice always imagined true romance would feel.

Her mother was angry, crushed, embarrassed. She was noisily horrified when Alice moved out — and yet the union took more and more definite shape.

When Rose was born, Alice struggled to keep up. Hers had never been a very order-conscious family; now her housekeeping, or lack of it, confirmed the heritage. The little house, not at all chic to begin with, was strewn with clutter and smudged with the smeary kind of dirt that comes from failing to clean surfaces carefully. Laundry and kitchenware were continually backlogged, giving the house an atmosphere of chaotic struggle.

Otherwise, Bob and Alice settled in and installed themselves in the Paris community as a more or less normal family. They had the usual amount of contact with her mother and Bob's mother, and some as well with Bob's older brother Cyrus, a local plasterer. In many ways theirs was typical of lower middle class life in the small cities of Ontario in the 1930's. The infant Rose was followed by Jay, and later by a third child, Frank.

But life, day-to-day, became more complex for Alice with each new child. Funds were scarce as the Depression drained the continent. Patience wore thin. Life was troublesome and annoying.

Still, Bob and Alice were making it.

Then a northern winter wind brought pneumonia to Paris, and Bob took sick. The illness seized him slowly, forcing him to bed again and again, and eventually leaving him there permanently. His lungs filled ominously with poison, choking off his air supply. His croupy cough echoed through the house, punctuating the crying of babies and the staticky noise of a cheap radio. Until one day.

There was very little money left to bury him properly. Bob's mother was hateful toward Alice and refused to offer any assistance. But Bob's older brother Cyrus, who was fond of Alice, gave her some help. He felt badly for her, left stranded and practically penniless with three children in the middle of the Depression. He had always looked on Alice kindly, if for nothing else than for what had obviously been great beauty not so long ago. Now, of course, her hair had thinned out considerably and the crow's-feet were creeping out from her eyes, but she was still a lovely woman in her early thirties.

And attractive, especially to a man like Cyrus, who had known marriage at one time, but whose wife had died tragically in a hellish neighbourhood fire years before. Cyrus had never had children, but he had wanted them. Now, at fifty, he felt that the opportunity for fatherhood might have passed him by.

Cyrus sat and mused about Alice in the days after his brother's death. He could feel his interest stirring as he thought about her, thought about accompanying her to town, dining out with her, engaging in light and lively conversation with her, laughing with her, living with her, waking up beside her...

In the earliest days of Alice's widowhood, Cyrus gladly provided the necessary tower of strength in her life. He tried to be as present as possible, filling in the emotional gaps as they became evident. She needed someone to talk to, sometimes more than at other times. She needed someone to listen to, where there had been someone for so long. She needed direction, and comfort, and support — and Cyrus provided all of that for her, willingly, in the days and weeks after the funeral.

At each turn, as he sensed her relying on him, he warmed up more to the idea of making her his own. And likewise, he felt more and more confident that she would indeed accept the notion. Look at her: she is smothered in children and house-keeping and financial need. A successful businessman in the community could solve most of her problems in a single stroke of the judge's pen.

And he, Cyrus — he could feel the old youthful urges blossoming up again inside him. In lovely Alice Peters Wick he could renew himself as a man, and father his own brother's children, and live the orderly, acceptable life of a fifty-year-old Canadian businessman.

But even as Cyrus Wick sat musing alone between frequent encounters with the object of his growing affection, the object of his growing affection was sitting alone and musing herself. Internally, she had fled from the guilt impulse for years, having trashed her spiritual heritage, burying her conscience deep in the daily routine of life. She had consciously dismissed the notion, again and again, that she had let her life be infected by sin. And yet the infection had spread, so thoroughly now, that it was hard to separate it from the stuff her life was made of. She surveyed the evidence: three children, a destitute financial condition (sadly symbolized by the stack of Bob's medical bills), a hostile mother-in-law, a hurt and broken mother (to whom Alice was an ever-present embarrass-ment), and a loveless life without God. And, as she looked around her, the house, she realized, was miserable — the final discouragement.

She had felt occasional longings for the old righteous life, but it was never practical to consider it after Bob came along, and even less so after the children came along. Now, for fleeting moments, she wondered if she could return...go back to the life she had known, freedom she had experienced but never fully appreciated — until it was gone. Now she had accepted a whole new burden, the burden of guilt and shame and of facing constant forms of disapproval.

Alice sighed and glanced at her children. They were the source of multiple pressures in her life. Besides mothering them, she was now being harassed by Provincial authorities to provide for them more adequately or risk court action. And, besides, the dark cloud of personal guilt, no matter how she tried to mask it, would always be hers to live under. And so, ultimately, what was the point of trying to go back? She could never really make it right, she told herself. It was already too wrong.

She could tell Cyrus Wick was going to make her an offer. She wanted to resist, to fall back and re-group and take God by the hand once again and live an upright life. She wrestled inside with the conflict. But Cyrus was so much security and good cheer. He was so much practical good sense. It was hard not to put her arms around him in tender moments, when he was being so kind and patient with her...

The conflict within her was not resolved by the time Cyrus finally asked her to marry him. It was tempting to accept for all the obvious reasons — even though he was twenty years her senior. But she wanted to flee at the same time, to run from the presssure, to escape the nagging Provincial authorities people, to set up shop with her children somewhere else, someplace where the past could be left far behind, someplace where the townspeople's tongues would not wag, where nobody would know the godly life she had once lived and would therefore have nothing to compare the present to — where she could tell a single, elaborate lie about her past and be done with it all.

People said there were a few more jobs available in the States than in Canada. Michigan was only a few hours away. She had two sisters in Flint. She could leave the children with her mother and spend a few weeks looking for work there. She could stake a new claim on life, and bring the children after her, and begin again, fresh and new and, for all practical purposes, clean.

Cyrus did not anticipate rejection. He had spent hours and days imagining Alice's tender, timid response — maybe she would even hesitate, and want some time to think about it, in a thoroughly charming and feminine way. But he never foresaw rejection. He was unprepared for what she said.

It stung when he heard it. He roared silently inside, like a wounded lion, equally angry and hurt. It was unconscionable that she would ever turn him down! He was especially peeved by the realization that his brother had been good enough for her and now he was not — a notion Cyrus created himself, although Alice never alluded to such a thought. And yet, Cyrus' exterior was gentlemanly. He nodded and said he understood, and lied that it was all right.

As she drove out of town, with trunks he had helped her to pack, he was smoldering inside, the snubbed lover. The smoldering and boiling did not stop as she drove out of sight; Cyrus continued to feed it by reciting the grating scenes in his mind: the vulnerable times, the tender times when he had helped her and encouraged her, and then the ripping moment when she so casually explained that no, she couldn't marry him. Every time he rehearsed the scenes, he grew more and more furious with her.

He had a great capacity for kindness; he had demonstrated that, and he had been cast off. But he also had a great capacity for revenge. This he — and Alice — would discover.

Alice fled to Flint, Michigan, hoping vaguely for her life to turn around, hoping specifically to put some distance between herself and her past.

Maybe, just maybe, she thought, she could finally get straightened out. Maybe a spiritual renewal would magically happen to her in a new environment, and she would suddenly begin living the kind of Christian life she knew was right.

But her spiritual roots had long ago been pulled up. She

was far removed from the foundation of Scripture that had once been the building block of her evangelistic ministry. Now there was no bedrock in her life — only running, fleeing, searching.

In Flint, one company making machine parts had survived the collapse of all the other machine parts companies. Irving Machine Parts was hiring temporary and part-time help — a far cry from most of the surviving businesses of the day, where No Help Wanted signs hung like tombstones outside front doors.

Alice was hired there. The men on the job rarely found a good-looking woman working in the factory. She was the rare exception, and they gave her the appropriate amount of attention, which she thrived on day by day, smiling prettily or coyly or shyly, depending on the whim of the moment.

There was one man in particular who caught Alice's eye. He worked near her in the factory, and it only took him a couple days to make a strong point of speaking to her. He was good-looking, with a strong, square jaw and prominent cheekbones, a healthy, ruddy-faced man with a keen sense of humour. His name was Maury Blair. She liked him.

They went to dinner a few times. Alice never mentioned her children back in Paris. She never mentioned Cyrus, left behind to stew. She did say she had been married, and that her husband died of pneumonia. But this Maury Blair was so pleasant, so free from Alice's complicated life back in Canada, that she did not want to take any chances of spoiling a relationship with him.

The relationship, indeed, did not spoil. As spring turned to summer in Flint, they grew fonder of each other, and spent increasing stretches of time in more and more intimate settings. In no time at all, the vague quest for a new upright life had been forsaken, and Alice fell thoroughly in love with the charming, fun-loving Maury Blair.

He had none of the roughness of Bob Wick, none of the aging seniority of Cyrus; and there was none of the paranoia of Paris. It was a delight to be with him, to talk and listen and laugh. They picnicked in the local forest preserve, and Alice floated in limbo, far away from the pressures and cares and worries that had driven her to Flint in the first place.

But life could only be pleasant in narrow interludes, as long as she continued running. As the days grew hotter, she came to the creeping realization that she was pregnant.

The anguish began to deepen within her, as she began to understand what this would mean to Maury Blair. She could ruin him — she could devastate him — if she presented him with this situation. And she loved him so much, she didn't want to see his suffering face when she broke the horrible news to him. She could see his laughing face turn somber, his bright, cherry eyes grow dim and sad...and then, in his upright, gentlemanly way, he would ask her to marry him. Which would bring up the question of the three children back in Paris, and the whole tangled story of her past.

Each day she stewed a little hotter, as the need to make a decision pressed down tighter and tighter upon her. She juggled the options in her mind, desperate for one of them to jump out as the obvious best choice. And meanwhile she prayed and prayed fervently that she would turn out miraculously not to be pregnant.

Maury noticed her growing restless, seeming troubled and sometimes distant. She could not keep her mind on a conversation. She was cross at times. But she kept insisting nothing was wrong.

Inside, she was bewildered. Life had turned on her once again. The pressure was on once more. She felt that soon the events would overwhelm her, and she would be thoroughly submerged in the tidal wave of bad luck and the horror of a tragic fate.

The rock of her salvation seemed so long gone, she could never turn back there. She could never lean on Jesus again. It was so remote a possibility that she never paused to consider it seriously. That was her youth; that was her childhood. It was Sunday school. Now she must cope as an adult.

And yet, she could not seem to cope, not quite.

She sat on the bed, and sadness washed over her. Her tired face grew red and hot as she wept. It was senseless to cry by herself, but the grief of her life had caught up with her again, and she had nowhere else to put it except into her tears. She did not

16

wail or moan. She only wept quietly, alone, hurting for herself, for her lover, for her children in Paris and the child within her.

And then, as she always did, she drew herself up with a deep breath, wiped her wet face with the back of her wrist, and set about to throw all the clothes back into her trunk. She must run again. She must flee the scene of the thoughtless, accidental crime. Perhaps, with one more flight, she could erase the mistakes that were dogging her trail.

She left no note for Maury Blair. She tried, but she could find no words. She could not bring herself to lie to him so consciously, so directly. Every lie was a new flight, but now she even fled from lying.

At least this is the story we heard later.

When she failed to show up for work the next morning, Maury sensed immediately what had happened. At the end of the day he went to her place and found it vacant. The ugly light began to dawn. He searched the room for a clue about her destination. There was nothing. Alice had said nothing about her plans. No one at Irving Machine Parts had heard a word.

The dull ache of panic threatened Maury's internal equilibrium. If she were carrying his child he wanted to know so, he wanted to marry her, to care for her, to provide for the child.

But he could not know for sure — not until decades later — that he was indeed my father.

CHAPTER THREE
Strike the Deepest Blow

And his mother called his name Jabez,
saying, because I bare him with sorrow.

— *I Chronicles 4:9*

CHAPTER THREE
Strike the Deepest Blow

She loved the child stirring within her, even as she nervously pressed the accelerator, pushing toward Paris, straining to think of another lie to explain the birth that would soon be evident. She loved the child, loved it because it was Maury's, and she had loved Maury. If only she hadn't had to ruin it.

But she must have a story — an explanation for the family and friends and wagging tongues of Paris. She must have a reason for the expanding abdomen that would soon force her out of her clothes and into the smocks of maternity.

She bit her lip and squinted down the highway, although she was not watching the road. In her mind's eye, Alice could see her mother's face, only slightly clouded over after so many years of heartache. She could see her sisters, turning their heads from side to side, considering her story, wondering, wondering. And she could play the scenes with the various neighbours already in the theatre of her imagination: the hypocrites would nod their understanding as they faced her, then sneer and giggle and lash out heartlessly as she walked away.

As the miles of pavement slipped away beneath her old car, Alice took the elements of truth that best produce lies and assembled her fable.

"I met a wonderful man in Michigan."

"Yes, Alice," they would say, or "Yes, Aimee?" from the ones who had known her the longest and still called her by her evangelism-days nickname.

"But of course those overnight courtships never work out."

21

"No, Alice, of course not," they would say, with less credibility in their voices.

"And we were divorced last month."

"Oh, Alice." "Oh, Aimee." "We're so sorry."

"Then I found out I was pregnant."

This was the line that would tell all — tell whether they bought it or not. She could tell by the narrow passage of time between her words and their response: if they failed to respond quickly enough, she would know her story had not held up. In that narrow passage of time, the tiny sliver of silence after she revealed her pregnancy, she would always know whether she had assembled credible details — or whether there was too much reasonable doubt in the known facts: that she had only been gone a very short period of time, and that no one had heard about this marriage back in Paris, and that she was coming back undeniably pregnant.

But the story, Alice realized as she wheeled the auto onto her old street, would have to do. It was all she had to go on, absurd or not.

She called herself Mrs. Blair, something that she felt gave her a reasonable amount of respectability. Mrs. Maury Blair. The name sounded fine to her.

But the story, she could tell each time she told it, was not being swallowed by the wagging tongues of Paris. No one laughed in her face — which was no surprise — but the gossip mill was heavy-laden for weeks as Alice's pregnancy became obvious.

Cyrus was waiting for her, open-hearted and — by all appearances — content to wait in the wings of her life. He meticulously pursued a comfortable, active social life, making her feel womanly when by any other standard she would not. It was a sexual investment for him — charms that would pay off later, he hoped, when this pregnancy was out of the way.

But she sensed an anger — somewhere deep inside him — about the earlier rejection, and about the child she was now carrying for another man.

Certainly by her own standards she did not feel womanly. Inside, Alice was in a tumult — the old desperation clung to her like syrup. She could not get away from it. The money problems were worse now than ever; she did not feel well much of the time; the children were irritable and reckless; the house was a disaster.

Some days, as she sat with her stomach before her, the child kicking relentlessly, Alice longed to see Maury Blair again. She had become engulfed in his warmth that summer, and now as the Canadian leaves went dry and brown and bland all around her, she missed him. There was not the same love for Cyrus that there had been for Maury. Maury had been, by the warped standard of her life, a real love. And yet she knew, even as she pined, that she had lost Maury Blair — forever. On some days she felt the strain would be unbearable, and yet she always awoke the next day, bearing even more. And she grew bigger still, heavy with the child of a man she truly loved, a child she somehow hated to be having — under these awful circumstances.

There was no money for a hospital visit, so when the awful day came, Alice called on Zeke Virgil, the pool hall owner, to drive her to Brantford, in Birch County. She could not ask Cyrus — it was somehow too unpleasant in Brantford, where destitute mothers had delivered many babies. It was not the kind of welcome Alice would have liked to give to the offspring of Maury Blair — in fact, she determined never to tell the child the truth about where he was born — but at least it was relatively safe, and she would be cared for in the crucial hours.

He was a sickly baby, never comfortable in those early hours and days of life with the environment into which he had been thrust — a foreshadowing, perhaps, of future agonies. He seemed to absorb germs from the air as if his system, in some perverse way, required them to survive. Every bug came to live in his frail little body. Baby fat was quickly used up, and his arms and legs failed to flesh out; they looked like rails.

Alice was dizzy with the pressures life had brought upon her, as she recuperated from yet another childbirth. Every new decision had to be weighed delicately against the mired backdrop of her past — and whom she had told what versions of the truth. Out of all of this, she concluded that the new infant must be named after the man she had lied about marrying and divorcing: the baby would be called Maury Blair.

But in her troubled confusion, Alice did not want to legally implicate the man she had been loving when she conceived this baby. So she avoided confronting the legal requirement — registering the child, to acquire for him a birth certificate. She did not want to list Maury Blair as the father. Because of this, although Alice had little understanding of the ramifications, little Maury Blair would have no legal existence.

She came back to Paris with the sickly infant, and the old familiar stirrings returned when she saw Cyrus again. There was still that twinkle in him that told her he was accessible, vulnerable, a possibility. She was careful, cautious in her approach as they dawdled over a beer at the Paris hotel bar. They gingerly made their way through the tense necessities — Alice advising him what a horrible mistake the Blair affair had been, how badly Blair had treated her (even though she had not told the rest of the townspeople this), how she had discarded the cad after only a short time in Flint. Cyrus resisted the notion inside, knowing better, but she was so coy in her appeal to him as they talked that he had difficulty measuring out the truth from the nonsense. So he nodded agreement.

But Cyrus did not plunge in. He wanted to string her along awhile, dangle her over the cliff for a bit. He loved the — penitent prodigal lover, returning to him on her knees, needing him, so badly, so pitifully. And he could hang her. He could pour all the anger and humiliation of the old rejection back into her now. The simmering, smoldering hatred within him — now many months in the making — could finally now, in this perverse way, find worthy expression. He thought about her weaknesses — the most vulnerable elements of Alice's fragmented life. He looked for a place to strike the deepest blow, to leave a wound that would not heal, but could only grow more painful.

And he thought of the baby, Maury Blair.

Her eyes always lit up just a bit when she looked at little Maury. He could tell she had reserved a special place in her heart for the child, and the thought of this infuriated Cyrus. It was clear to him that she still had a deeply rooted love for the man who had fathered the little bastard. Whoever that lover had been, he had found his way into Alice's bed in that long, humiliating summer of Cyrus' rejection. Cyrus thought about the child now, the living evidence of his own spurned affections, and he boiled silently with rage.

Then it struck him that his situation was ideal: now he could have his cake and destroy it too.

Somewhere in the night, Cyrus Wick arrived at his sinister plan.

"Oh Cyrus, you can't be serious," Alice chided him a little nervously when she heard his proposal.

Cyrus looked at her evenly, without any expression behind his eyes. "I am."

Alice felt the flutter of worry in the pit of her stomach. She knew instinctively that he meant what he said: he would marry her, but she must get rid of little Maury.

"Cyrus, he's just a child —"

Cyrus' face flushed and his nostrils flared momentarily. "I'm not gonna father that little bastard," he growled, his face reddening as he spoke. "Let someone else mess with him. I'll take care of my brother's kids and that's all."

Alice fell silent, her heart pounding. She raced through the complicated details of her life. She desperately needed the financial security that Cyrus could bring. She could no longer hope to care for so many children with virtually no income. She knew she could not afford to unravel the relationship with Cyrus for any reason.

But to give away her baby — Maury Blair's baby. The thought stuck in her throat. He was a narrow, frail little boy, nearing one year of age, and something about him brought a special response of affection out of her everytime she looked at him. His big eyes and his dark hair, so unlike her other children, so much like Maury's father...

Alice took Cyrus' big hand and stroked it gently. She needed to diffuse the discussion for a while. She was sure Cyrus would change his mind with a little more time, a little more affection.

Cyrus held fast. Days trudged into weeks, with the house and the children and the poverty and the squalor closing in ominously on Alice. She felt the cluttered rooms growing imperceptibly smaller each hour, the stench rising up out of the kitchen sink like a ghost. She relentlessly cultivated Cyrus, spending more and more time in his arms, prodding him with all her available charms to change the conditions he had established for their marriage. But Cyrus would not budge. The little Blair bastard would have to go.

And the time Alice spent in her own house, with her children, became more and more a mockery of motherhood. She had no money, no resources either financial or emotional, for caring for these children. And she had no hope of help through Cyrus as long as the little black-headed bastard — Cyrus called him the "black bastard" — was in view. Alice fled the warring emotions within her by retreating into a mental fog. Deep in that fog, she could sometimes consider the horrible alternatives calmly. She wandered mentally through a dozen different plans, each one ending with Maury's disappearance. Of course, the Provincial authorities could take him, although she had heard the horror stories about the wasting of little lives in that bureaucratic maze. More often her mental meanderings took her to unreasonable extremes, with scenarios of desertion and murder. There were certainly many ways to kill a tiny child. She imagined sometimes that she could actually do it.

One day she wrapped the baby and headed for his birthplace, Brantford. Alice's sister Isabel lived there. They would visit for a couple days. Alice needed to escape, at least for a little while.

The house stood in a rural setting, with fields all around. Alice said she was going to take Maury and go for a walk. Isabel puttered around the house until Alice returned, with the sun setting and the air turning cooler.

The baby was not with her.

Isabel, sitting at the kitchen table, looked up at her younger sister sharply. Alice only looked at the floor and muttered about the weather and the next day's meals, then sat down at the table and sighed heavily. The room fell silent.

"You can't do this," Isabel finally said softly. "Where is he?"

Alice could not answer. Her eyes were glazed and blank.

26

"Alice, I won't be a part of murder," Isabel said, with urgency in her voice. She slid her chair away from the table and stood up. "We've got to find him."

As her sister headed out into the fields, Alice sat alone at the table. Her head was swimming with pictures of Cyrus, the other children, the wreck of a house back in Paris, then with pictures of Mr. Maury Blair, and the innocent face of the helpless infant she had left in the high grass no telling how far away. She stood up and shuffled to the kitchen counter, leaned against it wearily, and waited. She could not tell whether to hope Isabel would find him or hope otherwise. Her stomach was slashing inside her. It could be an accident...no one would ever know...

It seemed like hours later that Isabel pushed open the back door and carried in a shivering child, wrapped in her shawl. Isabel's face was creased with lines and patched with red from the cold. But she had nothing to say to Alice.

Calmer the next day, Alice returned to Paris with Maury.

Alice struggled with the new child, and with her other children, to keep some semblance of order — or at least avoid outright chaos — in the cramped house. The air hung in the house like a heavy cloud, with the slightly unpleasant odor of an unkempt place. A naked, dingy lightbulb poked through the ceiling in each room, casting everything in the flat, harsh yellow of sixty weak watts. Cyrus' ugly offer stood. The bills piled up. The pressure continued to mount in Alice's mind.

Inevitably, she fled again, this time to London, Ontario, still resisting Cyrus' mandate to give Maury away. In her flight, she became pregnant a fifth time — a pregnancy draped in secrecy to this day.

The new baby, Mark, was born in Alice's despair. Sickly Maury, meanwhile, was registered as a patient in the same hospital, under treatment for multiple illnesses. Years later, the hospital's record books would reveal that the infant Maury Blair was visited by someone who signed in as Mr. Maury Blair. The visitor's actual identity may never be known.

Alice languished in her unhappiness, feeling bewildered and pitiful. She knew where she would have to come to rest, where she would finally have to settle if she was to keep life from consuming her entirely. She knew she would have to return to the drab, ugly past — little different, actually, from her drab, ugly present — to Paris, to face the townspeople one more time, to see the hard-edged Cyrus Wick — and perhaps negotiate an arrangement of some kind with him. After all, with Maury a little healthier now, perhaps Cyrus would reconsider his harsh decision.

She felt the need to mend, to take some time and just heal over. She had been ripped and shredded and hurt too often. It was telling on her. She was only in her thirties, but she felt old.

She thought about Cyrus. Could she love him, in spite of what he was demanding? Could she build a relationship on the slim thread of affection they had felt? Sometimes, she mused it was possible.

Once again she hobbled to Cyrus. She lamely asserted that her flight to London had been necessary, and indeed therapeutic. But Cyrus snorted with derision. She was not her old smooth self, able to lie with finesse. She was a beaten, troubled woman, and Cyrus, sensing her desperation like a lion preying on wounded zebra, raked her mercilessly for the one concession he required: if she wanted him to rescue her from all this, if she wanted him to marry her and father her children, the black bastard must go.

Alice struggled not to explode in tears, but she had too little strength left. She caved in and cried with anguish. He was killirg her.

But her life had taken such perverse twists and was by now so horribly distorted that she could still at least consider his awful counter-proposal. In some moments of far-fetched imaginings, it seemed so senseless to strangle her own life, and the lives of her other children, for the sake of this one scrawny little boy. If she could only bring herself to give up this one, all the others would be taken care of. It would be so simple to put that distance between herself and the cause of her problems — little Maury Blair.

And the problems were mounting, even as they seemed to

be bulging toward some cosmic limit, some boundary beyond which no one person's problems could ever mount. As she looked out through her jaded eyes, she saw an unreal world. Life shrieked at Alice every moment of the day, through an unreal haze, with every blink of her eyelids, with every simple action and reaction. She felt herself being jabbed and prodded continuously, and her mind swirled with images of disaster. She had to get relief. She had to get some peace. She had to get some help. She had to get Cyrus Wick. Who else would have her? Who else could ease the pain, dissolve the trauma? Sometimes, as she tried to pull together her swarming thoughts, she boiled the conflict down to a single, simple option: she could either give up Maury, or she could go completely mad.

She accepted the offer as they nursed beers in the bar one evening.

"I'll do it," she whispered.

He looked at her.

"Hm?" he grunted.

"I'll let Maury go," she said softly, her eyes shut tight against the sound of the words.

Cyrus was silent for a moment, then exhaled noisily.

"Well, see that you do," he said, looking away with caustic nonchalance. "We'll get a marriage license tomorrow."

Alice sat motionless, suspended in sadness. She swallowed nervously and wondered if she would really do it.

CHAPTER FOUR
"I'd Kill You If I Could"

> I think we are in rats' alley.
> Where the dead men lost their bones.

> — *T.S. Eliot, 1922*

CHAPTER FOUR
"I'd Kill You If I Could"

Uncle Bill was a barber. He used to come over on Sunday afternoons for dinner, and afterwards he cut the kids' hair.

I listened from the vent in the floor upstairs, smelling the hot foods and cuddling up to the sense of security it all seemed to provide.

And when the haircuts were done, the dialogue rarely varied.

"Well, Alice, why don't you bring Maury down," Uncle Bill suggested, "and we'll cut his hair too."

Cyrus growled angrily at his older brother. "No way is that black bastard getting his hair cut."

"Oh come on, Cy," Uncle Bill chided, "you crazy old bugger, let him come down."

Cyrus cursed and refused.

"He'll probably turn out to be the best damn kid you have!" Uncle Bill teased.

Cyrus exploded into fits of cursing. Uncle Bill was not intimidated.

"Ah, lay off the kid, Cy."

"One of these days, "Cyrus shot back in a gravelly voice, "I'll kill that black bastard."

I shivered when I heard him, but I knew I was safe on Sundays. The old man never beat me when Uncle Bill was in the house. And in a moment when Mum could slip away quietly, she advised me to drop by Uncle Bill's barber shop on my way home from school the next day.

"Get out of there as quickly as you can, though, Maury," she told me. And I could see the sadness in her eyes.

She found ways to avoid sending me away in the early days of her marriage, hoping that Cyrus would grow accustomed to my presence. He did not. He fumed incessantly whenever I was in view, cursing and growling like a chained alley-dog. I never had an earliest recollection of his beating me; I could only remember being beaten, always being beaten.

Cyrus drank heavily as Alice's accumulated problems now became his own. He stalked home from the tavern in the hotel downtown and fixed his drunken rage on me. While I was still an infant, Mum sometimes wrapped me in blankets and walked the streets carrying me, waiting for Cyrus to spend his anger and collapse into a drunken sleep back home.

I learned to walk in time to learn to run. He would grab me by the arm and begin pounding on me, until Mum could get to him and pull him away. If I squirmed away myself, I would eventually have to encounter him again, and I learned that late payment was more severe than immediate payment. I learned to go limp and let his big fists strike me at will. If I could not run to escape his noticing me in the first place, I could not run at all.

Patterns emerged as Cyrus' alcoholism drove him to deeper and deeper hatred of me. As the dinner hour approached, he walked the same route home from work, via the tavern. I established hiding posts — a fence, a bush, or my favourite tree, just outside my solitary window — where I could conceal myself and watch him coming. I trembled as I peered out, gauging his drunkenness by his gait. Every evening I had to decide whether or not to slip home ahead of him by way of my well-worn short cuts. If I was home when he arrived, I could be beaten ferociously — if he were in that frame of mind. I tried to determine by watching him secretly on his way home just how miserable he was, just how bad he was feeling, and just how likely he was to head straight for the bathroom or the bedroom once he got to the house. His drinking created terrible digestion problems for him, which sometimes forced him to skip my beating.

On some nights, too, he was simply cranky, wanting his supper and wanting it now, rapping his cup on the table for a refill of tea, and looking around with a scowl and saying, "Where the _____ is that paper I brought home?"

34

But usually, if he were just uncomfortable enough to be enraged, I could be certain of a beating. Sometimes I decided to stay out, to hope that he would forget my absence and pass out for the night. I found places to sleep around the neighbourhood — under a veranda, beneath a porch, in a thicket, or simply on the frozen earth of a neighbour's lawn or an empty lot. Many times a concerned neighbour would rouse me and take me inside, my teeth chattering and my flesh trembling with the cold; the neighbours knew full well that my fear of the crazed Cyrus Wick had kept me from going inside.

I never sat at the dinner table with the rest of the family, except on those rare occasions when Cyrus was not home for dinner. "Let that black bastard starve," he snorted when one of my brothers mentioned me as I listened from the vent on the landing upstairs. When they could, one of them would slip a few scraps of food to me afterwards, like impish teenagers feeding the family mutt on the sly. Sometimes, they couldn't.

And every evening as the dinner hour neared, the trauma began all over again. I could wait outside and face the weather and the horror of hiding — and hope that someone could sneak me some food — or I could go inside, in to the physical warmth and the frozen emotional tundra, and face my chances with Cyrus.

If I was in the bedroom as he came in, the terrible countdown began as I heard him push his way in the front door downstairs. I stood in the darkness, having learned that it infuriated him to see me enjoying a normal lamp-lit room. I only tried to hide under the bedcovers one time. Bunched up in a terrified ball in one corner of the bed, the electric terror pulsing through my skinny frame, he lurched up the stairs and into the blackened room. It was too dark to see anything, but Cyrus did not turn a light on. Instead he began to hunt and search and curse in the darkness, groping wildly along the walls, under the bed, and around the edges of the bed.

"I'll find you, you black bastard," he said over and over between his gritted teeth. "And when I do, I'll kill you."

My mind raced desperately. If I kept silent and hidden, he would eventually find me, and I knew he would beat me harder and longer for having to ferret me out. But I could not squeeze out a cry. I could not make myself call out to him and invite the horrible abuse.

Suddenly I felt his hot fingers make contact with my ankle.

"I've got you now, you black bastard," he growled like an animal.

He yanked me off the bed with a single snapping motion. In the next split-second, I could see him silhouetted against the moonlight in the window, his fist rising up above his head. I closed my eyes and waited for the blows to begin.

Each impact crushed my face or my arms, until I felt myself fading away. The images and thoughts began melting together as I struggled to maintain consciousness. I could hear the voice of my brother Mark, as he clung to Cyrus' pantleg, pleading with him to stop. But he pounded me again and again and again, then kicked me to the floor, then began punching me again. I could feel the cold wooden floor beneath me, and then the freezing steel bed frame against my face. Cyrus rared back and unleashed a final solid blow to the back of my head, and I was gone.

I awoke to feel the aching pulse throughout my body, beginning in my face, where my skull had been butted up against the bed frame. My little brother Mark was cradling my throbbing head in his arms, looking down into my lumpy, bruised face.

"Maury," he said softly, "are you all right?" I mumbled something through swollen lips.

"Maury," Mark said in a terrified, breathy voice, "I thought you were dead."

The revenge instinct fed his alcoholism, and his drinking heightened his thirst for revenge. They said he had suffered a terrible wound in World War One — a bullet ripped into the corner of his eye socket and passed through his head and out the back of his ear — but there was no evident scar. Some said he went away to war and came back a different person, somehow warped by the countless killings he witnessed as he crouched in the foxholes and scrambled for survival. Now I seemed to be the target of his irrational anger. He could never be satisfied with the damage he inflicted on me, and he only stopped beating me at the very last moment, when he could not be sure of sparing my life. Then he would finally drop me to the floor and lumber away, still cursing and still reminding me, "I'd kill you if I could, you black bastard."

But I was only the victimized symbol of Cyrus' hatred. The real vengeance he sought was against my mother, Alice. I was the child she had loved, the offspring of the man she had loved — the man she had fled to and clung to instead of Cyrus, in that impassioned summer so many hot summers ago. She was horrified in the early days, when he first began hitting me, and she always scurried to my defense, pulling me away from him and shouting down the old man. But as the years dragged by, her defenses sagged. He wore her down by his sheer consistency, by loading her up with insults of her own, calling her terrible names. She grew tired and numb, hopelessness seeping in.

Life had never lightened up for her. The children she wanted Cyrus to care for were victims in their own ways as well. Rose, Jay and Frank knew the old man as Uncle Cy, although everyone called him "the old man" behind his back. They kept him at a distance, ignoring his rages and despising him generally.

Times were tough for all of us. We boys slept together in one bed, with only Jay in a bed of his own as the oldest. Additional brothers Cyrus Jr. and Hal were soon added to the family, and we lay across the bed the wrong way to fit everybody in. Sometimes my brothers hid me under their bodies when Cyrus was on a late-night rampage. Sometimes it worked.

Across the landing, the girls' room was only a little better than ours.

Baths were rarely taken. There was no tub in the house. Changes of socks and underwear were an unknown commodity.

Instead of baths, we had "the end." Our house stood on a ridge beside the river. The ridge was supported by a cement wall, which ran in either direction away from our place. At one end of the wall, the river had eaten away the cement, and the weakened structure had corroded and collapsed into huge chunks of concrete, which stood in the river like stubborn soldiers refusing to give up the fight. We often played among the rocks at "the end," the closest we came to regular bathing, rarely thinking to remove our shoes and socks to keep them dry. With no dry replacements available, we simply threw the damp articles in the corner as we went to bed, and pulled them back on in the morning, musty and damp after a cold night, musty and stiff after a warm night. During warm weather my feet grew sore for weeks at a time as I unwittingly administered the constant punishment of "the end."

Each child was responsible for his own laundry; it rarely got done. When enough students had harrassed me and enough teachers had sent notes home to my mother begging her to wash my clothes, I sometimes scooped up a few belongings and headed down to the river, where the town's children were accustomed to swimming. With red-faced shame, I scrubbed my clothes, while other kids jeered as they played in the water.

We were the children other mothers advised their children not to play with, the family that the rest of the neighbourhood wished were not there.

And they looked at me. They knew I had somehow managed to be singled out by the old man as a target of continual wrath. One day the old man marched home, livid with rage, belching his liquor and spilling obscenities with every breath. He lurched down the cement steps behind the house, down into the cellar, snarling curses, and seized his ax by the handle.

"Where is he!" he shouted as he huffed and puffed back up out of the cellar. "I'm going to kill that black bastard! Where is he!"

I had seen him coming down the street, sensing his unusual level of fury. I was hiding behind a hedge outside, and now I could see him elbow his way out through the back door, clutching the ax-handle and looking wildly from side to side.

"Come here, you black bastard!" he roared as he headed my way.

I felt the shock of terror ripping through me, and for a brief moment I watched motionless as he stumbled in my direction, the ax blade glistening ominously. Then, suddenly, as I realized he could cut me to pieces, I squirted out of my hiding place and flew down the street. He kept roaring angrily as I put more and more distance between myself and the terrible menace, until finally I had ricocheted into someone's backyard, breathless and frightened and trembling, sobbing with fear. The neighbour lady poked her head out of the back door, her face drawn together into a tense frown.

"Maury!" she hissed. "Come inside!"

She hid me for the night. The old man finally gave up the manhunt and crashed angrily back into his house, where he vomited loudly and passed out.

I never knew the history. I never knew why he had singled me out, why the hatred was focused on me. I knew only the hatred, and the feeling of being unwanted.

There is an inbred impulse in a child that longs for love, reaches out to security. When that reaching impulse fails to connect, it backs up inside the child like clogged sewage. Day after week after month, I felt the frenzy of unwantedness. I groped to understand it, to find out why this hunter hunted me. But I was too terrified, too fearful of my very life on a daily basis, to ask anyone. I could only interrogate myself, miserably, in my solitude. And the anguish built up and found no relief. I was a trapped rat, and there was no escape from the frothing revenge of the old man Cyrus Wick.

When Mum was gone, to a sister's house or her mother's house or to visit a neighbour, I agonized for my safety. And yet, eventually, I came to understand that Cyrus would never harm me when she was not around to hurt over it. It took years for me to fully understand the ugly dynamics of their relationship, but Cyrus had no need to lash out at me unless it could serve his sick and twisted purpose: to teach Alice a lifelong lesson of abject anguish. When she was within earshot, he rarely failed to abuse me, to point again verbally to that great crime she had committed against him — rejecting him and taking up with the mysterious Maury Blair. He taunted her in big ways and small. When the other children were handed ice cream on the lower level, Mum tried to wrangle a portion for me as I lay on my stomach at the air vent on the landing.

"Oh," she led off smoothly, trying to grease the chute, "let's take some up to Maury."

But Cyrus could not resist the bait.

"Maury! Give that black bastard some ice cream?" he snarled, scraping his chair away from the kitchen table and rising up like a grizzly roused from sleep and unhappy about it. "Where the hell is he?"

And he headed up the stairs, cursing as always, vowing to kill me. I leaped from my place on the floor and slipped to the far window of the bedroom, awaiting judgment. But Mum came after him, pulling him away and ridiculing him as best she could to draw his attention away from the target. Grumbling, still miffed, Cyrus reluctantly stopped on the landing, pulled his arm away from her angrily, and muttered a few final obscenities at her before clomping into his bedroom and dumping himself into the unkempt bed.

But it was all she could do. She could only on occasion stay his hand. The wall of revenge could never be scaled, not by any human means. Cyrus' distorted anger had built it too high, too thick. Mum could never throw a birthday party for the child of Maury Blair, never express any open affection toward me — for fear of making a holocaust even more ferocious than it already was.

Only one weapon could cut through the worst of times and bring a temporary halt to the fury: the name of Jesus, employed in something other than a curse. Cyrus mounted the steps at the end of a rainy spring day, vehement and noxious. He failed to make the turn on the landing, and lumbered straight ahead to grab me out of my desperate little corner. He struck blow after blow, until finally he was fed up. Then he picked me up with his two monstrous hands and thrust me through the bedroom window.

I hung in his grasp over the rain-swollen river below, which ran along the ridge just behind our house. I screamed, terrified of the fall and the water, but I was afraid to kick or squirm away. The dreadful vice-like fingers of Cyrus Wick were my only hope for survival.

Mum heard the screams and came up the stairs. She stood

in the doorway only for an instant, in virtual disbelief, then marched toward Cyrus with a fierce maternal determination. She sank her fingers into the scruff of his neck and said, "In the name of Jesus, pull that boy in and put him down."

Her words were like bullets, clear and distinct. Cyrus froze. I could feel my heart pounding through my rib cage, waiting for movement, any kind of movement, something to tell me if he would toss me into the water like a scrap of garbage — or whether he would obey the unusual authoritative command of my mother.

After an endless fraction of time, he drew me in back over the window sill and let me drop to the floor. He would not look at Mum, but instead muttered a filthy word under his breath and stalked away. Mum waited for him to leave the room, then she turned to me. I was picking myself up, shaking badly, longing for her to take me in her arms and convince me it would never happen again, that she would protect me from the old man from now on.

I wanted so much for someone to love me.

But she patted my shoulder and looked at me with her big, sunken, doe-like eyes, eyes that declared her sadness but failed to console me.

And once again, the question that sounded so terribly absurd: "Maury, are you all right?"

She barely waited for a response. She couldn't afford to. If she lingered with me, the grizzly would return. She knew it as well as I did. There would be no stolen embrace, no furtive moment of affection for the child. She was suffering hell herself. And she had been trained to avoid the black bastard.

Until, one spring day, she sent me away.

CHAPTER FIVE
Fragments

> We make war that we may live in peace.
>
> — *Aristotle, circa 375 B.C.*

CHAPTER FIVE
Fragments

Word flashed through town that a convict had escaped from one of the nearby penitentiaries. Some insisted that he was holing up somewhere in Paris. It was the greatest excitement of the week, as housewives gathered over afternoon tea and their husbands elbowed up to the town bars to discuss the most titillating news that had cropped up in months.

And every tiny sound in the night simply had to be the con.

I lay awake, between my brothers, trying to get comfortable, trying to sleep, if only for lack of anything else to do with myself. Suddenly I heard a loud knock outside, and we all jumped. I could hear my mother speaking to the old man. She had heard a sound in the backyard. The terrible truth suddenly flashed through all our minds — the con was on our property!

There was little hesitation on Cyrus' part. He was too vicious to lie in bed waiting for someone to sneak in and attack him. He bolted out of bed and charged down the steps.

As soon as he was out of earshot, we all tumbled out of the rickety bed and squeezed around the window. I pressed my face against the dusty glass to get the best possible view of the action. From our upstairs perch, we could look down and see the dark figure of the old man charging out of the house, his fists closed and ready to hammer his victim to a pulp.

I thought about the poor escaped convict, and I felt sorry for him. If the old man ever caught him, I could imagine the con fleeing in a panic, welts and bruises and cuts all over his body. In my mind's eye, I saw him running headlong back to the detention center, banging wildly on the front door, pleading hysterically for the warden to let him back in, promising never to escape again after meeting that monster in Paris.

We found out later that the con was recaptured miles away. He had never come to Paris at all.

But unlike the imaginary convict, I had no prison to prefer. There was no escape. Suspended in the limbo between unwantedness and deprivation, I found no resource but the hateful, tempestuous old man who served as its hub. There were no options — no source of dinner but the sporadic source I had always known, no other source of shelter but the house I was sometimes able to sleep in. In the winters, when I found myself outside instead of inside on a cold, windy evening, I leaned against the house and let the tears freeze on my blotchy face. I had no evidence of my own badness except for the constant indictment of the old man's vulgar threats. I did not know why I was so despicable. And in my helpless state, as a bewildered, anxious child, I cried out to the vague image of an Overseer, who I desperately hoped would hear me someday: God.

The local Pentecostal church had welcomed us to their Gospel Cadet meetings, even though we were preceded by our smell and followed by our filth. The church was only a short walk from the house, just up around the corner, and perhaps because they found themselves in the same unfortunate neighbourhood as we, they welcomed us on Friday nights. It was a madhouse, with games of all kinds to drain the energy out of the dozens of street kids who assembled there, then Bible stories and choruses. The leaders, all nameless to me and seemingly identical in their scrubbed cleanliness, were kind and patient — knowing, I always thought, what was going on back there in the Wick house.

And I heard them talk about God. I had no reason to believe it was a lie. I never saw Him, and really heard no explanation for that phenomenon, so I never considered meeting Him, never thought about establishing a personal relationship. But they talked to Him, and they said He could help people when they had problems — and so my primitive prayer life was established. Leaning on the south wall of the house to avoid the worst of the winter wind, with the peeling paint scraping off onto my threadbare shirt, I cried and I called out to God. I felt overwhelmed, and hopeless, nevertheless.

Mum had moments of genuine concern about our salvation, but the brave, bold lady evangelist "Aimee" of years before had vanished, replaced by a confused and fearful woman. Once in a while she herded us to the Pentecostal Sunday school. We attended without shoes rather than wear the rags we owned. But our attendance was sporadic at best. Occasionally she gathered us around her and told us Bible stories, but there was no clear-cut evangelism. She was a masterful storyteller, capturing our attention with her wide eyes and expressive voice. In those magic moments we were transported to another world, another life, and introduced to the strange and mystery-draped characters of the past. Ironically, I was most fascinated by the story of the two women who asked King Solomon to settle the dispute over who had mothered the surviving baby between them. Pretending to be equitable, the wise monarch ordered that the child be cut in half and shared equally by the two women. But the real mother, in her love — and according to Solomon's good gamble — preferred to give the child up rather than see it senselessly destroyed.

Although I had no way of knowing it yet, my mother had made the opposite decision. Unable to part with her infant, she had chosen instead — by default — my virtual destruction. I was the child in dispute, being torn in two. Cyrus was the sword. There was no wise Solomon to make the best decision — nor, in fact, any decision at all.

Mum's sporadic storytelling sessions accomplished no change, produced no hope, for the fragmented family. Even as I acquired my own first New Testament, when the Gideons came to school to make their usual presentation, the event was more marked by humiliation than by hope.

The Gideons had carefully engraved the name of each student on his personalized pocket-sized Testament. As the organization's representative called out the names, one by one my schoolmates marched to the front to claim their prizes. I felt my heart beating a little faster as the A's were dispensed with and the B's began.

Then I heard the terrible mistake.

"Mary Blair?" the man called.

I was horrified. The class exploded with laughter and catcalls.

"It's Maury Blair," I corrected him lamely, my face burning with shame.

The rest of the class carried their Testaments home with them at the end of the school day. I went home empty-handed, to face the hell the old man would once again bring with him. Days later, my corrected New Testament would be handed to me privately after school. I rarely read it, and failed to understand the stuffy King James dialect when I did read it. Not till years later would its impact be felt in my life.

People were concerned, people were praying for me — but I never knew. The leaders at Gospel Cadets, suspecting some of the turmoil in our home, were praying for all of us. People driving by our house, or driving by as we hitchhiked from place to place with our mother, prayed for us throughout the years — but seldom stopped to help. Across the river from our house stood a mill. The workers watched us on their breaks as we cavorted in our steep backyard, riding the flimsy fence at the edge of our little yard, threatening every moment to go tumbling down the ridge into the river, or tobogganing down the ridge on scraps of cardboard. Some literally watched us grow up on the river bank, and wondered how we survived.

During moments of relief, on long summer days when school was out and Cyrus was safely cloistered in someone's house with his plastering business, the rigid fear exploded free and took form in wild play. We played frenetic hockey with a tennis ball in the front yard. Our property became the neighbourhood boxing ring or baseball diamond. We brought mounds of dry leaves from neighbours' yards and dumped them in our yard to play in. The old man came home swearing every time. "We don't have a tree on the property," he fumed, "and look at that mess."

My brothers and I excelled in neighbourhood terrorism. Next door, the notorious Mrs. Dudley became a favourite target. We climbed her trees against her wishes, knocked out her windows playing baseball, and kept her generally aggravated. Beyond Mrs. Dudley's place was the Michaels residence, also a favourite playground, where our mischief was commonly rewarded by an angry Mrs. Michaels stomping out onto her front porch, wagging her finger in consternation. Across the street were the Hartmans, whose daughter Donna inspired us to rock-throwing and other guerilla tactics. One old grandma lived down the street; she sat on her veranda and resolutely ignored us as our rock-missiles bounced all around her. We called her the Old Hen. (Years later I would learn from a relative of hers that she had prayed for me fervently and faithfully in spite of the harrassment.) And the ridge over the river bank was the perfect castle wall when anyone plunked down to do some fishing: we showered them with rocks. At least one mother on our street warned her children: "If I ever catch you talking to any of those Wicks, I'll whale tar out of you."

There were dangers in our wild kingdom, however. I located a group of burly workmen constructing a veranda, and found a perch above them, from which I could bounce rocks off their hard hats. One of the men, irritated, stabbed his shovel into a mound of soft earth and hurled it at me. At the same moment his gloves slipped off his sweaty hands, and the entire shovel sailed up at me. I had no time to dodge the blade. It smashed into my forehead and split the flesh. I tumbled off the perch and instinctively scrambled away, blood flooding down my face. I came to the door of my house, breathless, and then realized the trouble I could get into if I bled in the house. I could imagine Cyrus grabbing me and pounding me, shouting curses, if I bled on the floor. Dizzy and desperate, I knocked on the door and then backed down to the ridge, kneeling with my bleeding wound held well out over the edge.

Mother came to the door and reacted with alarm. She led me to the kitchen sink and began to wash the blood away, only to find that the bleeding had not slowed.

"Oh Cy," she called nervously into the living room, "I can't get the blood to stop."

Cyrus sneered. "Ah, let him bleed to death."

Mother wrapped my head in a towel and hurried me to a doctor, who administered the necessary stitches.

Whenever Mum was not at home, it was usually to visit her sisters in Flint. Invariably she took my brothers Mark and Cyrus with her, leaving me behind and terrified. It was the most painful rejection of all — but Mark and Cyrus were younger, and she did not trust the old man to take care of them. I sat in my bedroom for hours, looking longingly beyond my favourite tree and toward the train bridge across the river, the last place I could see the train as it took my mother and brothers away. Inside, the emptiness ate me alive.

But during Mum's absences, the strange metamorphosis never failed to take place. Cyrus never hit me when she was gone. Why expend the energy, when hurting Alice was the whole point?

The abuse, though, was always just as vicious as ever. When Mum left money with my oldest sister Rose to take us all to the circus as it came to town, Cyrus intervened.

"You're not taking that black bastard anywhere," he told her.

"I am, Uncle Cy," Rose pouted. "Mum left enough money for me to take him."

Cyrus grew madder by the moment as Rose held her ground. I listened to the unfolding drama from my place next to the floor vent upstairs, my stomach tight with tension and hope, until finally Cyrus grew tired of the sparring, and settled for hateful acquiescence.

"All right," he growled, "take the black bastard — and throw him over the bridge on the way home."

There were desperate, futile attempts at manliness. The vines down at "the end" were submerged in the spring, but as the river ran shallower in the summertime, the slender cane weeds were exposed to the hot sun. I found that I could break off a dried cane and light one end and it would glow like a cigarette while I sucked on the other end. But the manly experience took its toll. I smoked the cane down completely and spent the entire next day vomiting up my nausea.

By the fifth grade I had graduated to stolen cigarettes, which I carefully hid from my mother and my older sister Rose. When I ripped my coat and asked Rose to mend it, she smelled the telltale odor.

"I smell cigarette smoke," she said with a frown as she sewed.

"Really?" I asked in my best nonchalant voice.

"Maury, have you been smoking?" she quizzed me suspiciously.

I pretended to be aghast at the very suggestion. "Who, me? Naw! Not me!"

There were occasional triumphs. I found I could play a good game of softball, and I became captain of one of the school teams. We called ourselves the Indians, and my brother Frank made us colourful cardboard arm-bands to declare it.

But baseball in the street was too lowly, too common to afford true heroism on a continuous basis. For all the thrills of playing well and winning, my ground-level perspective on life kept me from feeling fabulous about it. Only once did the sport elevate me to the heights of giddy self-fulfillment. Bases were loaded with two outs. I came up to bat, and something magically charged me. I deliberately let the first two strikes zip by me. Then, in a brash gesture, completely beyond the realm of my puppy-whipped character, I pointed boldly toward deep center field, Babe Ruth style.

The kids on both teams laughed and booed and hooted at me, but I was resolute. The pitch came, I threw myself into the swing, and the softball rocketed up and out over the far edge of center field.

For a brief moment there was stunned silence. Then my teammates cried out in complete mania, whooping and cheering, exploding with the gleeful surprise of the impossible beautifully accomplished. As I trotted around the bases, following my three teammates, I felt the flush of sheer single-handed victory. It was such a rare high, though, that I hardly knew what to do with it.

And there was always the old man to bring me back down once I reached the house.

If softball provided any emotional cushion to life, the classroom punctured it. I had no security blanket at home, and the thought of going to school terrified me from the beginning. I could not conceptualize a place of fun or freedom or fearlessness, because from the point of my earliest memory I had known none of these. With exceeding terror and nausea I approached first grade, my mind full of dark images: a huge brick building, with a clone of Cyrus at the chalkboard in every classroom, snarling and snapping.

Once the initial adjustment was made, however, I found that the schoolroom could be a source of more attention than I had ever received in my short, unhappy life. I learned quickly enough that the kids around me giggled and approved of me when I deliberately botched up my schoolwork. The teacher saw through the ruse and strapped me soundly. I quit going for the laughs and withdrew into a lonely shell, unable to make friends by any other means.

On a day when the upper grades had vacation because of teachers' conferences, I walked to school downcast. My older brothers Frankie and Jay passed me in the back of a pickup truck, hitchhiking a free ride just for the fun of it, and I felt myself wanting to cry in my loneliness.

The loneliness festered hostility within me. Two colleagues and I had been run out of class and determined to gain recognition by sneaking back into the classroom and startling the old teacher. As we crept up the aisle, she looked up suddenly and jumped with fright. We squealed in laughter. She grabbed me by the arm and shook me violently. Instantly I lashed out at her.

"Get your filthy hands off me," I spat.

And I broke away and ran full-tilt for the stairway.

As I raced down the stairs I came face to face with the principal, staring me down for my speeding violation. I turned back to go up the stairs and found myself cut off by the infuriated teacher looking down at me from above. Panicky, I clutched my stomach and screamed, "I'm sick!" and fled past the principal and out of the building.

When I got home, my mother dutifully made me return to school. Soon I was sheepishly facing the teacher again, expecting to be whipped severely.

But the punishment was miraculously spared.

"Maury, I could give you the strap for this," she offered quietly, "but it wouldn't help. And I know you're having a difficult time at home."

It was an embarrassing way to let me off the hook, almost worse than getting the strap, for it told me she knew the grueling humiliation and mental torture I was being subjected to. It made me all the more distant and withdrawn to think that the people in town could see through the terrible truth: I was a rat, trapped in my own house.

But it was evident. The terrible truth always had a way of poking through. I ran down a staircase in the school building and tripped, falling headlong into a brick wall. I was knocked unconscious, and as I awoke from the haze with teachers and students huddled around me, I instinctively covered my face with my arms, kicking and fighting to escape. "What's wrong with you, Maury?" they asked as they tried to calm me. Suddenly I realized that Cyrus was not beating me. I had no answer for their puzzled questions.

Escape was a constant challenge. There were dozens of trivial, unrelated efforts. I found washers in the gutter and wore them like treasured rings. Marbles recovered from sewer holes became prized possessions. I admired a boy named Terry who lived down the street, the son of the Old Hen, one of our favourite neighbourhood targets at rock throwing time. Terry enjoyed wild flowers, and I ambitiously pursued the same interest for the summer. I found a plot of suitable earth beyond the fence on the ridge behind the house, where Cyrus was least likely to look. There I planted an assortment of wild flowers, collected from various exotic locations all over town, from alleys to rich people's gardens. Like the single-minded gardener stereotype, I lost myself for hours in the pitiful little garden, huddled over my watering and puttering as if mine were competition-bound blooms of the finest varieties.

With excited patience, I sat still long enough on the back steps to get robins to take scraps of bread from the ground right in front of my feet.

And I made friends with a field mouse, feeding him scraps of food and taming him sufficiently to have him running up and down my arms and in and out of my tattered pockets. I kept him in a makeshift cage near the garden — until one day a heat wave rolled through Ontario and the tiny prisoner died of thirst. A lump forced its way up into my throat as I looked down at the stiff little animal. But I would not let myself cry.

Summers had another peculiar tragedy: Cyrus was inclined to take off from work early on summer days, head for the tavern in the hotel, and become ferociously inebriated. His erratic schedule made it more difficult for me to gauge his frame of mind; sometimes I failed to post myself in my hiding places if he headed home ahead of schedule. And often he caught me downstairs — the ultimate taboo — which guaranteed more hideous cursing and more vehement beatings.

The tension seemed to swell with the seasonal changes. Summer simmered things in our house, until on many occasions my mother farmed me out to trusted neighbours for a day or two at a time — to let things cool off, to assuage Cyrus' vicious fury. There were not many neighbours inclined to take in such a rank little ragamuffin, but folks from the local Pentecostal church could be relied on to treat me well if they could be persuaded to take me at all.

The separation from the familiar — in spite of the horrors of home, disturbed me. I never felt at ease in anyone else's home. One night my mother had installed me in the house across the street. I lay in the prescribed bed alone, a luxury of sorts, except that I was nervous and fidgety. The foreign atmosphere — the relative cleanliness, perhaps, or maybe just the suggestion of unwantedness that the whole thing represented — kept me awake and troubled. And then I heard the sound of a mouse gnawing under the bed. My pet mouse had given me no great love of wild mice, particularly one gnawing, uninvited, under me in the middle of the night.

The man of the house stopped by my room to check on me and found me out of bed and dressing.

"What are you doing?" he asked, a little startled.

"I'm going home," I replied with determination. "I'll take my chances."

He tried to talk me out of my decision, but I could not stay there. I was too flighty, too disturbed to settle in, even for one night.

The man knew what I would face at home. "How will you

get in?" he asked.

"I'll find a way to get in."

In moments I was standing at the front door, peering up at the bedroom window directly above it. The house was entirely dark. I knew if I awakened Cyrus I was dead.

In a shrill, hoarse whisper, I roused my mother: "Mum! Mum!"

I sighed with relief when she slipped silently into view in the window. She understood immediately, and calmly signaled for me to be quiet. Then she disappeared, and in a minute she had pushed the front door open to me, stealthily. I sneaked up to bed.

For once, I had gotten away with something under Cyrus' nose.

But all the pressures finally took their toll, and I began to be dogged by horrible nightmares. Two predominant themes recurred, night after night, and I was powerless to stop them. In one ghastly sequence, I was being sucked into a swirling black tunnel. Someone I could never see was waiting at the end of the tunnel to crush the life out of me. I clawed and screamed and tried to hang on, avoiding the end at all costs — until I awoke quaking with fear, afraid to go back to sleep and the possibility of facing the tunnel again.

On other nights I found myself floating helplessly down a river. Stretched across the width of the river was a long rope, with a ghoulish tangled knot in the middle of it. The knot was alive, seething and breathing, anxious for me to be drawn into it, so it could destroy me.

Sometimes lions chased me; other times I simply ran and ran and ran to escape an unknown predator. Again and again I awoke screaming, or lay screaming in my sleep, my mother trying to sooth me and shush me to keep Cyrus from exploding in the next room.

My mother needed relief as much as I did. Often Cyrus took perverse delight in sitting across the kitchen table from her cursing at her and calling her ugly names, threatening to beat her if she got up and left the room. She sometimes sat for hours at a time, through the night absorbing the abuse, tears angrily refusing to spill down, even though her heart was aching.

She had to steal money out of his pants pockets at night to buy groceries.

He had made her a wench, forcing her to grovel.

There was a spring when Cyrus was especially violent, when Mum was especially fragile, when the summer sun began baking Ontario especially early, and life became a sweltering pressure cooker.

Mum knew I might not last the summer. She never said anything about it, but she looked at me and looked at Cyrus and knew instinctively that it would be a terrible season for all of us.

When she told me she was shipping me off for the summer to Lud and Selma's farm down toward Toronto, the hysterical silent screaming began inside me and continued unceasingly. I was aghast at the thought of leaving my home, the gruesome household that was the only source of any semblance of security that I had ever known.

Why would she do this to me?

My unposed questions cried out, shrill and relentless, as I watched her pack my hopeless little wardrobe into a cardboard box and prepare me for the trip.

And I knew, as if I could look clearly into the future, that my nightmares were about to become reality.

CHAPTER SIX
Strange Kinships

> One would be in less danger
> From the wiles of the stranger
> If one's own kin and kith
> Were more fun to be with.
>
> — *Ogden Nash, 1945*

CHAPTER SIX
Strange Kinships

It was the serene, bucolic stereotype of a Canadian farm, complete with barn and horses, chickens and pigs, Lud and Selma and a grandmother. To survey the scene would tell any observer that this was a place of uttermost peace and thorough tranquility.

But I saw it all in shades of ominous gray. It was eerie and threatening and dangerous to me from the moment I stepped on the property.

Lud, a friend of Cyrus' family, was larger then Cyrus, well over six feet tall and nearly twice as broad, with bulging muscles, an unsmiling brute of a man. Selma was continuously annoyed, a complaining shrew who found me to be a nuisance and nothing more. Grandma was the self-appointed disciplinarian, wagging her self-righteous finger at every turn.

The farm, for all its charm, was an uncomfortable place for me, leaving me ill at ease, as if I were wandering through some ill-fated Hitchcock movie. When Lud beheaded chickens, I could hear them helplessly scratching on the inside of the pail, their nervous systems expiring in frenzied fits of kicks and tremors. I shivered. The sound seemed magnified in my mind, the claws of the chickens scraping metallically against the inside of my skull.

The grandmother, still the supreme spiritual voice of her family, grew angry with me at the dinner table one evening and suddenly rose from her chair. She pulled me away from my place and yanked my trousers down to my ankles. In front of the two others, she spanked my bare bottom, then stood me in the corner to stare at the wall. I stood in a trance of shame, mortified with the humiliation, longing to go home — unsafe or not.

And the telling trial of the summer: chronic colitis destroyed my digestive process and all hope of controlling my bowels.

Although Cyrus and I had no blood link, it almost seemed as if his awful digestive problems had been handed down to me, as if by sheer meanness he could transfer to me the worst possible inheritance. From my earliest childhood, my intestines, prompted by nervous tension, knotted up stubbornly, only to relax capriciously, without the slightest warning. I scrambled for a bathroom every time, but generally I arrived too late. Then, red-faced, my composure devastated, I peeled the filthy underpants off and washed myself at whatever facility I could find — a faucet, a water pump, a creek. At home I found the most convenient route was to run down the ridge to the river bank, even though I often encountered other kids swimming and playing there who never failed to hoot and jeer as I did my dirty work.

Now, at the farm for the summer, with no explanation for what my body was doing to me, I found myself more nervous — and more prone to such problems than ever before. As long as I could get away with it, I hid my dirty pants under the bed in the room where I slept, until Selma finally searched out the source of the stench and furiously washed them all. Soon Lud stepped into the picture, angry with me for upsetting my hostess, and declaring unilaterally that this was "just a filthy habit and nothing more." He warned me sternly not to let it happen ever again.

It was, however, literally out of my control, and the inevitable inevitably occurred.

The brutish Lud seized me by the neck and lifted me clear off the ground. As I dangled like a rag doll, he stomped out of the house with me, toward the great circular rain barrel out back. My stomach grew squeamish as I saw his purpose unfolding before me. Standing next to the barrel, cursing me ferociously, he thrust me down into the barrel with a single violent motion, submerging me completely in the cold water.

My mind spun wildly as I struggled to hold my breath. His strong fingers were pressed solidly into my neck and shoulder; I could not escape if I tried. The full terrible range of possibilities flashed through my head, including the ultimate: would he just kill me right here, like this?

My lungs began to burn, aching for oxygen. I could feel my pulse in my temples; I could listen to the death knell as it pounded through my skinny body. Wave after wave of terror and nausea swept over me in rapid succession, and my lungs felt like they would explode if they didn't get nourishment.

Then, suddenly, his fingers tightened and pulled me out of the barrel. As my face broke the thrashing surface of the water, a gulp of air rattled into my gaping throat. I coughed and sucked for more air desperately, but before I could recover he had pushed me back down into the water. Again he held me under until my chest ached for relief, and again he hoisted me up at the last possible moment. I had barely filled my lungs with a swallow of oxygen before he had thrust me under the water for the third time, and then a fourth time.

Until finally he felt he had made his point, and he set me down with a jolt beside the sloshing barrel and walked away.

"See that you break that filthy habit," he muttered as he stalked up the porch steps and into the house.

I wobbled and sat down roughly in the dirt, leaning against the barrel, too traumatized to cry, too weak to stand up and wash my sloppy underpants.

It was strange, but I would be glad to go home.

Two friends wandered into my troubled life, each destined for a tragic farewell.

Skipper was the illegitimate offspring of a Labrador retriever and something else, a big, bony, black and tan dog who appeared out of the proverbial nowhere one day and apparently sensed in me a certain bastard kinship.

He was never my pet, only my buddy. I never put him on a leash, and yet he stuck with me as if he had been expertly trained. It was a loyalty born of common commonness, magical and unshakeable. We ran together, played together, and even though Skipper occasionally disappeared to sow wild dog-oats in parts unknown, I was always sure of his return.

It was instinct, then, that told me something was wrong. The air turned bland and still around me, and I knew in my gut that it was a problem with Skipper.

From face to face I bobbed, throughout the neighbourhood, asking every friend, every aquaintance, if there was any news about Skipper, any information, any ideas.

Someone said he had been taken.

I suspected from the beginning that he had been an owned dog at one time, although I had never seem him tied up or in anyone's care. Now, perhaps, the Humane Society had picked him up and sold him — or perhaps he had simply been pressed into slavery by some evil human master.

Old Ed DuPuy, the story went, had Skipper tied up in a shed behind the Wincey Mills where Ed worked, across the Nith River. If I stood on the ridge behind my house, I could see the top of the shed where Skip was supposed to be.

I knew if I whistled for him, he would answer me. It was the whistle we always used, three short shrill tones, and as they echoed down the ridge and across the river, I strained to hear the response.

The wild, frustrated barking broke back across the river valley. My heart flopped, delighted to hear the old familiar sound, despondent with the mystery so sadly resolved.

Each day for a week, I took my position on the ridge and whistled out the signal to my old friend. Each day, without fail, Skipper barked wildly. I could image him straining at the chain, his neck muscles pulling against the choker, his paws scraping at the earth. But to no avail.

Finally I had to see him. I had spent too many hours peering grim-faced across the river, and the mental pictures had worked on me until I had to take the chance. Early in the evening, after the day shift had shuffled out of the Wincey Mills, I sneaked around behind the little shed.

When he saw me, he bounded to me, a gleeful puppy once again, if only for the moment. I hugged him as if he were a long-lost brother, home from war.

But I could not free him. It hurt me not to, but too many people knew we had been inseparable, and I would only have to turn him back over to old Ed DuPuy if I slipped away with him now.

Hot tears stung my eyes as I held Skipper for a final moment. Then I walked away from him, agonizing. He strained at the chain, trying to follow. But I left by myself.

There was an older boy named Bill. He had no last name for all I knew. He hung around with kids younger than he. His pants were too short, exposing ugly sores on his legs. He was the sullen enigma that every town has and doesn't care for, as mothers wonder what he is up to and how he is influencing their children.

He had been rejected at home and spent most of his time sitting on curbs in neighbourhoods like ours in Paris, talking in low tones to the few who would carry on any conversation with him.

As a fellow reject, I became one of the few.

One day we looked across the river, silently, at the train bridge. In the warm autumn air, with the leaves dying their beautiful autumn death, it was a moderately inspiring sight for two oddities like us.

Finally Bill quietly broke the picturesque silence.

"How would you like to go for a ride on the train, Maury?"

I looked at him in disbelief. I had never had such a stupendous offer in my life.

"Gee, I'd like to," I answered breathlessly. But I could still hardly believe it. "You mean a real train ride?"

"I'm going tomorrow," he responded casually. And we arranged a time, the following morning, when he would come by, and I would be waiting outside the house for him.

I was still astonished as I lay in bed that night, staring into the ceiling, imagining the powerful chug-chug of the great engine as it vibrated the floor of the train car beneath me, imagining the fall leaves whisking by and stirring up in miniature tornadoes as the huge wheels of the train thundered down the track through the woody areas.

The next morning found me waiting for him in my little red cotton coat, on time. He came by as planned, and I fell into step alongside him, soon working up a little sweat to keep up with his long-legged stride.

When darkness finally overtook us, we collapsed under a tree in a random yard. I was tired, worried, and weak from hunger; we had not eaten since we left.

I had a hard time falling asleep, the unfamiliar surroundings triggering my nervous system. As I lay awake in the grass, a shuffling silhouette appeared. Alarmed, I squinted at it. It was a grisly old hobo, his clothes disheveled and his whole appearance creating the impression of abandon and hopelessness.

I was frightened by the old man, but he did not stop to bother us. We were just a couple of hobos ourselves, as far as he could tell. And he was essentially correct. He kept moving along.

Finally, I fell into an uneasy sleep.

Back home, Mum had realized my absence and had begun the inevitable search — slowly at first, sure that she would locate me in some typical place, then with a more and more urgent pace, as it dawned on her that nobody had seen me all day.

Perhaps it would have solved some of her problems to be rid of me, but her maternal instinct did not allow her to arrive at that conclusion. She loved me still, in her own sorrowful way. Furthermore, Cyrus had demonstrated his true character in such a vile and consistent way over the years that Mum had little hope left for him ever to reform, even if I somehow vanished.

The likely point of disaster, everyone knew, would be the river. Finally, Maury had slipped over the ridge, over the cement wall, and plunged to an awful death in the waters of the Nith. My brothers and sisters scrambled along the bank, peering intently across the river for my pitiful red cloth coat.

A local radio station began broadcasting my description, urging the townspeople to be on the proverbial lookout. A troop of Boy Scouts fanned out to make a search of their own, each perhaps hoping to get a badge of merit for finding the body. Several people joined in the boy-hunt. But the hunted boy was not to be found.

By nightfall, Mum was despondent.

"Good," Cyrus grunted when he heard I was missing. "I hope the black bastard is dead."

Bill and I set out to cover more ground on the second day. I was deeply worried, wondering where he was taking me, how I would ever get home, and what Cyrus would do to me when I got there. But we trudged onward anyway, and I remained silent about my fears.

"Hey! Where ya going?" a man shouted from his house as we walked through his neighbourhood.

"Woodstock," Bill called back.

The man was walking toward us, smiling broadly. "Hop in my car; I'll take you to Woodstock."

I was grateful. My legs were sore. As I settled into the upholstery of the back seat, I could feel my narrow muscles beginning to relax — finally.

We sat in his driveway for a long time, waiting for him to come back out of his house and get us on our way. Then without warning, a police car pulled into the driveway beside us.

My heart pounded as the policeman jumped out of the car and threw open our door. Before I could react they had dragged Bill out and stuffed him in the squad car.

"Are you all right, son?" he asked me in a friendly tone as he turned back toward me.

My eyes were wide and worried. "Yes, I'm okay", I told him. But I was scared.

We were driven to the police station and taken inside, where I began insisting that I had to get home. The chief of police was gentle with me. "It's okay now, Maury," he assured me. Then he turned to Bill, cursed him angrily, and demanded to know what the devil he thought he was doing by kidnapping a child my age.

"Well, he didn't have to go," Bill whined. "He wanted to."

The chief, red-faced with anger, abruptly kicked Bill in the rear end.

My mother was mourning, sitting at the living room window, holding my little brother Cyrus, when she saw a police car pulling up the street with my worried face pressed against the glass. Startled, she stood up, losing her grip on little Cyrus, who tumbled to the floor and cried loudly. Mum dashed for the door to greet me.

It was a good feeling to be missed, something I had rarely felt in my life. She poured a big bowl of porridge and set a huge Danish pastry in front of me to fill my empty stomach. I was worried about the old man, but it was Saturday, and Mum assured me he was over at the hotel, drinking, and could be counted on not to show up for a while.

Bill disappeared forever, a victim of his own loneliness.

Cyrus was disappointed to discover me alive and well. He was especially cranky for the next few days. I was particularly careful to stay out of his way.

But Cyrus was growing old.

CHAPTER SEVEN
Fail and Farewell

> At mealtime come thou hither,
> and eat of the bread,
> and dip thy morsel in the vinegar.
>
> *— Ruth 2:14*

CHAPTER SEVEN
Fail and Farewell

And as he grew older his powerful body slowly began to break down. By the time he had lived his sixtieth year, the decades of careless alcoholism had weakened the vital organs, and his energies sagged. The walk home took longer, the digestive system provided more spiteful and erratic performance, the liquor was harder to hold down. You could hear him breathe if you sat in the same room, as the lungs required more and more help to do their job. He sat often, more out of general fatigue now than out of the old boorish laziness, and for hours he sat in his slippers, aimlessly working crossword puzzles out of the newspaper. The hair had thinned, even to some extent in the nicotine-stained mustache.

He took a less taxing job as a spinner at a textile mill, but Cyrus still missed days of work nursing sore joints and muscles. What once had been simple, and merely a diversion on the way to the tavern, now became a complex, troublesome effort — and the tavern a mandatory recuperative stop. Then, after the tavern, the endless vomiting, sometimes all through the night, and to recuperate from that, a noxious mixture of vinegar and raw eggs. Money — even the money Mum ferreted secretly out of his pockets at night — became more scarce.

Mum saw the dilemma approaching afar off, and the old fleeing impulse rose up again within her. She had to quell it deliberately. Only because she too was tired and older and worn down did she not automatically dash away from the trouble like a scared rabbit.

The restaurant, then, was Mum's idea. Someone was selling it, and she decided we could buy it and run it as a family

— an absurd notion, on the surface, given the history and the dynamics of our particular family. And yet none of us considered that. We only heard that we were buying a restaurant and, because we had not learned to exercise preferences, we followed accordingly.

In a restaurant, one could live without the old man. He could spin as many days as he was able, sleep as many days as he needed, and the restaurant — in theory — would supply the financial needs of the rest of us. That my mother, after a lifetime of flight, could not realistically hope to succeed in her first such rooted venture, was never discussed. She had worked here and there as a waitress in restaurants and coffee shops around the area, a month here, a few weeks there, when times were especially tough and the work was available, and she felt comfortable taking on a restaurant operation.

But we would live above the restaurant, in an apartment that normally housed the owners. The house on the ridge would have to be sold and vacated.

It was the scene of so much hurt, the catalyst of so much trauma, I should never have minded leaving it. In every corner, in every shadow, I saw tragic memories. And yet, with my threadbare sense of security, this was my familiar world, the womb in which I had found the only nourishment I had known, even tainted as it was.

I was glum the day we moved out, as the years swept by once again on the movie screen of my mind. For a brief, glimmering moment, each event was called up, displayed, and then replaced by the next — each brutal beating, every surreptitious meal, every riotous round of play with my brothers in the yard...and I recalled those moments of revelation, when I began the long, tortuous process of learning who I was.

Mum could not remember when my birthday was, not for certain. She had gone to Brantford on that day in a panic of personal turmoil, and she could never remember whether it was April 27 or 28.

Children ask such questions as part of the natural course of growing up, and although Cyrus never allowed a birthday party or even acknowledgment of any sort, I found as a child that everyone else at school knew their birthdays, and I wanted to know mine as well.

Mother made the mistake of wavering. Caught off-guard by the question in a moment when she was concentrating on something else, she was not prepared to choose one date over the other arbitrarily.

"April 27...28," she responded without thinking. "No, 27."

"Which is it?" I quizzed innocently.

"Oh, Maury, it's not important," she answered, finally realizing what she had done.

I couldn't get any further with her. She dodged and ducked, never looking in.

My schoolmates found it ridiculous, a great source of fun, that I "thought" my birthday was April 27 or 28. When I had a sufficient amount of shame and embarrassment over it, I resolved to do what my mother had not been able to do: I decided arbitrarily on Wednesday, April 27, and then pretended with gusto that this was indeed the accurate date.

I was a circus freak to my schoolmates in other ways as well.

"Hey, Maury," the teasing question always went, "how come your older brothers and sisters are Wicks, and your younger brothers and sisters are Wicks, but you're a Blair?"

I had to get an answer from my mother, for I had to have an explanation for my classmates.

It must have been a piercing question for her, a question that dredged up decades of dirty linen, stirring all the ugly past to the surface of the emotional pot. She had mucked up her memories with layers of lies, and after so many years she could no longer recall precisely what story she had presented to whom, nor exactly which of her distorted relationships would be best served by various versions of the truth.

She sighed heavily as I looked into her big, once-beautiful eyes, tired and heavy-laden with years of hurts.

"Just tell them," she told me, "that I was married three times. And you were born to that middle husband."

"But what happened to the first two husbands, Mum?"

"They died, Maury. Your father was a hero and he died in

the World War.''

As a child, I could accept the story. As I grew up in the real world, I began to see how implausible it was. But quizzing Mum was as painful for me as it was for her: her response, when I cut too deep, was to retreat into self-pity, making me feel guilty for casting dark doubts on her past by even asking such questions. It was skillful defense, in a way, for it avoided the pitfalls of cross-referenced lie-telling.

But she made errors sometimes anyway. Remembering the shame of her speedy return to Paris from the States when she was pregnant with me, she advised me that I had been born in the U.S. — Byesville, Ohio, she said, a small town in the east central part of that state. She had actually never been there, and perhaps chose the town at random from a road map. But to her mind, an artificial Byesville heritage would separate me from the painful reality — that I had been conceived in fornication and delivered in furtive shame.

Now, as I stood on the street watching the old house being emptied of its contents, I could see all of us in all those awkward times, coping with the discrepancies.

On the street, my half-brothers and half-sisters defended me, as we all defended each other, against the nasty insinuations other children often made, quick as they were to repeat stories they heard their parents telling about ''those Wicks'' around the dinner tables of their homes. We brothers in particular took the classic familial gang approach to growing up, punching the day-lights out of rivals, particularly when one of our own number was threatened. I, for one, was not above taking on little girls as well. When I was in first grade, my little brother Mark reported tearfully that a girl in my class had hit him. Puffed with anger, I marched up the street to her house. She was raking leaves in her front yard.

''Did you hit my brother?'' I demanded fiercely. ''If you ever hit him again, I'll punch you!''

''If you take one step toward me,'' she shot back at me, ''I'll hit you over the head with this rake.''

''You,'' I sneered in return, ''haven't got the guts!''

And I took the forbidden step.

She swung the heavy metal rake clear over herself and

landed it teeth first over my head. I ran home screaming, blood running down my face.

In moments when the burden of the truth was not being brought to bear, there were times of great cameraderie among the Wick children with the odd Blair brother. When one of the neighbours inexplicably asked my mother if she could give me a little red wagon, we had to keep the information from the old man — but thrilled as I was to receive such an incredible gift, I was not one to keep such a delight to myself anyway.

My brothers and I piled into that new wagon with a hilarious vengeance, pushed and pulled and rolled ourselves all over the neighbourhood together, as brothers will. Likewise, when measles overwhelmed Paris, all of us took it together. The city put quarantine signs up all over the front of the house, with all of us cloistered inside like sickly monks, until the plague passed.

Only Cyrus' invective separated me from them in any way. On Christmas morning, Mark was always the first to awake. He brought back the report from downstairs: who got what, how much stuff was assembled around the tree. We shared the squealing delight — until the rest went downstairs. Then, because of Cyrus, I took my position at the vent in the floor, smelling the turkey, listening to the laughter and the oohs and aahs, the excited chattering of children with new playthings, hoping that someone would bring me a little something of my own.

And then, a week later, we brothers faced the New Year's Eve ritual together. Mum and Cyrus always went partying together, leaving us all home together. But before they departed, Mum lined us up to give each of us a kiss.

I was always squeamish as she came to me. I had never known her embrace, nor any physical expression of affection, and to have her kissing me now was disturbing. I squirmed, but she grabbed my head and gently pulled me toward her. I turned just enough that her kiss would land on my cheek. It was as much as I could take.

And then, with parents out the door and the pressure off, we threw our own New Year's Eve celebration, complete with mad-dog pillow fights and screaming and chaos. For a few brief hours, we enjoyed unadulterated exultation and wildness. Then, as the dawn approached, we scrambled to clean up our holocaust.

The makings of our many holocausts were now being forlornly carted out of the house and dragged downtown, to the apartment above the restaurant. When the place was virtually empty, I wandered around inside for a while, feeling an odd emptiness inside myself that matched the echo of the stripped rooms. I was very much the displaced thirteen-year-old, wondering vaguely what would happen now, now that we were leaving our old neighbourhood, now that we were going to run a business, now that the old man was so sick...

It was more of a task now, wreaking revenge on Alice's black bastard. It was something quite different to throw around a gangly bespectacled thirteen-year-old than it had been to throw around a slight, underweight seven-year-old. As nature had increased my height on a normal schedule, Cyrus had accelerated his own deterioration by sloshing huge quantities of liquor into his system. He could still work up the energy to curse me and hurl verbal obscenities, but the obscenity of physical abuse became more and more difficult for him.

I looked at the staircase, the one he had climbed so often to do me his particular injustice. My eyes followed it up to the bare bulb at the top, sticking out of the wall, its pull-chain dangling limp and straight, the chain that the old man had tugged so many times on his way down the stairs, leaving me in the dark and alone. I stared at the vent in the floor, the channel of light that I had taken as a friend, now about to be abandoned forever. For all the aching sadness of those hours on the floor, peering through the grating at the activity below, I still felt a void as I thought of leaving it behind.

The old man could be avoided now. He was slow to move, his anger reflex now spongy, where once it had been rigid. Now, if I simply stayed out of his way, I could move a little more freely in the house. But now, when freedom began to peek through, we were leaving the house. I would never know what freedom could have felt like there.

We called it Wick's Slop Shop, which infuriated Mum, for she had duly named it Wick's Restaurant. It was a typical greasy spoon joint, with booths on either side of a long narrow aisle. She had borrowed to buy it and renovate it. I swept floors and washed dishes and waited tables, along with my brothers and sisters, with all the solemn seriousness of the Marx Brothers. Our white coats and uniforms were a poor facade for our zany frolicking.

When our friends came in and put money in the juke-box, we showed them how to make the thing work for nothing. We gave school buddies credit for purchases, never expecting — and never getting — payment.

I was to start high school the month the Slop Shop opened. There was no decision to be made, as far as I could see. School was doing me no visible good, the restaurant could be fun to play with, and my family — a casual revelation — needed me.

Four months passed while I got away with it. Then a former classmate of mine got caught working without a permit to quit school, and he spilled my beans to the truant officer.

"Maury Blair is doing it! Why can't I?"

The chief of police came snooping around, and when I defied his orders to return to school, I wound up in front of a local judge.

"You're so young," the judge said, sounding genuine in his concern. "Your marks are good, and you've got potential. You should be in school."

I told him I was needed at home, but he didn't buy it. Reluctantly, bitterly, I returned to the classroom.

On my birthday I slipped into a new legal bracket and decided to try again. I applied for a chore boy's job at the mill and got it, but I still needed the chief's approval to quit school legally. With my principal's sympathetic backing, I went to the chief of police and made my plea.

He said he would think about it and let the principal know. I could check with the principal on Friday.

I had to start work on Monday, and I felt the tension building. My situation was preposterous. I had no money for textbooks, my pants were far too big for me, I never took off my old army jacket because I was ashamed of what I was wearing underneath. Other students laughed at me constantly for my appearance of utter depravity. I had to get out and get to work.

As I sat and stewed over the coming confrontation, I grew angry. Before leaving for school on Friday morning, I filled a pocket with alleys, big metal marbles, and determined to use them if the principal bore bad news. I knew they would throw me forcibly out of school if I hurled a handful of alleys into a teacher's face.

It was the last day I ever spent in high school. I had been released.

CHAPTER EIGHT
Wretched End

To the last moment of his breath
On hope the wretch relies;
And e'en the pang preceding death
Bids expectation rise.

— *Oliver Goldsmith, 1764*

CHAPTER EIGHT
Wretched End

The exodus had begun, and it was irreversible. My sister Rose, the oldest child, had left home to marry. Jay and Frankie each made their exits when they turned eighteen; each joined the Canadian armed forces. With each trip home on leave, and with each farewell as leave expired, there were the painful, teary scenes with my mother. She missed them, as she missed Rose, after so many years with them about the house, and she was haunted furthermore by the life she had managed to provide them while they were under her care. In their absence, she felt a sorrowful void.

With all the normal physiological pressures of adolescence, I responded to the evacuation by draping myself in teenage depression. Finally graduating to a room of my own by the sheer attrition of my brothers, I spent much of my time sitting in it, alone, listening to a radio. My mill buddies drank, but I never developed a taste for it after seeing and suffering the effects of it in the old man for so many years. But I was eventually able to smoke freely, and the air in my room became stale and gray.

Occasionally the lifeless life seemed worthless as well, and I muttered suicide threats to the only safe audience I had: my younger sister Sharon, who was growing up with a loneliness similar to mine, and who could be trusted not to repeat my words to Mum. "I'm going out," I told her, "and I don't care if I ever come back. If I have my way, I'll get killed in a car wreck." But the car wreck never happened. When I tried to force myself to push the accelerator and fling myself into a tree or over a bluff, something withheld me, something I marked down to childish fear and grew further depressed by. An invisible hand was restraining me, but I was unable to recognize it as anything but my own weakness.

Distant and restless, I searched out sullen diversions. I was intrigued by the boxing art, often listening to the boxing matches on Zeke Virgil's poolroom radio on Friday nights. A guy could box locally if he were sixteen years of age; at fifteen I lied about my age and began boxing. Strangely, boxing brought out Cyrus' only expression of interest in me, in a single, rare moment. Mum unexpectedly reported that Cyrus could show me a technique to help me with my boxing. As I watched, bewildered by the demonstration, he showed me how to throw a punch with the heel of my hand to save my knuckles from damage. For a few ironic minutes we threw imaginary punches at each other to practise. Then, it was over, as suddenly as it had begun. And the scene was never repeated.

I was bad at boxing nevertheless. My vision was poor, and I could never see punches clearly. Smarting and bloodied, I got out after a few gritty months of it. Cyrus' feeble expression of concern had failed to produce anything more than confusion in my mind.

The poolroom filled many of my evenings. One could be as quiet and sullen as he cared to be around a pool table. There was none of the required socializing of so many other sports. The pool hall became a sort of cocoon for me as my monotonous teenage years dragged by.

There were odd, undisciplined releases, reminiscent of the madcap rock-throwing excursions of years past. As a teenager, I was given to driving through the nearby Christian campgrounds with my buddies and hooting at the girls and shouting wisecracks at the "holy-rollers." I watched dozens of altar calls without the slightest understanding of what they meant. Invariably, we all told grossly exaggerated stories at the mill about what we had witnessed: a guy climbing a telephone pole shouting, "I'm coming, Lord!" was one of our favourites.

But most of the time I was in the shell, shooting pool at Zeke Virgil's pool hall in a glum shroud of silence, with only the clacking of the smooth balls and the small talk of the other players to break the monotony.

It was such small talk that one day cut through my sullen shroud.

"Yup, I remember the day you were born, Maury," the crusty Zeke Virgil offered one day when the awkward subject of birthdays came up.

I wasn't sure, but I thought he might be telling the beginning of a joke. I half-smiled and replied, "Oh yeah? How do you remember that?"

"I drove your mother down to a house in Brantford to have you."

"Not me, you didn't," I insisted as I felt an uncomfortable stirring inside.

"Sure!" he insisted. "I've known you since you were that big!" And Zeke held out his hands to show how big.

"Impossible," I retorted, aghast. "I was born in the States."

All eyes in the pool hall had shifted around toward the two of us, and now I was uneasy in the glare of attention.

"You were not," Zeke answered, his brow furrowing. "You were born right down here, outside of Brantford. You'd better go home and check with the old lady, Maury. I know for a fact I drove her to Brantford that night you were born."

My face was red with embarrassment.

"What's the matter with you, man?" someone jeered from a corner of the room. "Don't you even know where you were born?"

I pretended not to hear the remark, even though it had stabbed through the place like a knife.

"Come on," I muttered as I stiffly chalked up my cue. "Let's play."

Before long I had made a feeble excuse to leave early. I had to get an answer to the new quandary.

Still smarting with humiliation, I walked into the apartment and dropped myself into a chair at the kitchen table and looked squarely at my mother.

"Where was I born?"

She responded the same calm way she had always responded to this question.

"In Ohio."

I sighed.

"Well, that's funny," I replied, the edge of sarcasm rising in my voice, "because I was just down at the pool hall and Zeke Virgil says he drove you down to a house in Brantford the night you had me."

I watched her face. She looked down quickly, her eyes clouding over as the murky past once again drifted into the present. Her instincts began trying to construct an alibi in her usual old way, but within a second or two she knew she would have to confront the truth this time. It had been a stupid, needless lie anyway.

"It's true," she responded softly.

But she would answer no more questions for me. She was too empty. The recollection of those ancient pressures was more than her emotional framework was willing to withstand. When I asked her for details, she was silent. Her own abuse of me — the emotional violence of these endless untruths — would continue.

I sat alone for an hour, just trying to absorb the revelation. I was Canadian. I had no birthright anyway, and no traditional ancestry, and now to discover that I had been imagining my citizenship as well!

I sucked in a long, slow breath of cigarette smoke. I didn't know quite how to feel.

Cyrus continued his decline. Eventually I found myself slouching in the chair next to him, watching the fights and the hockey games on our run-down black-and-white television set in the apartment. We rarely spoke, except to exchange comments about sports personalities or teams and their relative worth or worthlessness. But for all the hours we logged together, with Cyrus guzzling beers and the two of us smoking innumerable cigarettes, we never opened up a line of communication. I was far too old to beat, he was far too sick to rail at me with his former passion. But now there was no reasonable alternative — so we sat in silence.

For me, it was as if we were growing closer. I had never known this sensation, the sensation of being tolerated, and I interpreted it as relationship. Over the final years of his life, I actually grew to feel close to him, even though there was precious little evidence of acceptance.

Cyrus was still, and ever, the complainer. "How the _____ did I ever get mixed up with this bloody outfit!" he often shouted when his irritation level crept high enough. He saw himself as a victim in life, set upon by fate to carry the burden of this odd family and the full complement of financial troubles. Wallowing in this nasty brand of self-pity, he sank lower and lower into ill health.

The foreman at Penman's Textile Mill grew irritated with the old man. He was getting so sickly and missing so much work. The apartment echoed with his cackling cough, the gutteral noises of a man slowly dying.

When his fragmented family could no longer provide enough immediate care, Mum and I helped him to the car and drove him to the hospital. We were met at the door by a white-uniformed nurse with a wheel-chair. As Cyrus awkwardly dumped himself down into it, I felt a rare and curious sort of pity, a humble hurt for this once-giant ogre who was now too weak to shuffle down the tile hallway under his own power. I pushed the wheelchair myself, and my mind turned with the big spoked wheels. He had been so strong, such a bulwark of awful power, and even after the years of hateful beatings I somehow admired his strength. Now, looking down over his bald head, I could see the feeble veins in his arms, the deep wrinkles in his hands, the loose flesh hanging on a once-mighty frame. I felt sorry for him.

Medical science brought too little expertise too late. The assorted poisons of alcohol and hatefulness had done their irreparable harm, and the degenerative process was irreversible. Discomfort decayed into agony, grumbling into silence. He lay in the hospital bed, the sheets stretched across him like the wrapping of quiet surrender.

Mum and I visited often. He was always conscious, making it an even more pitiful sort of death. I sat and listened to the occasional cursing and groaning. It was such a change from the roaring of years ago. He was so helpless, so broken. Mostly, though, we sat in silence, listening to our own heartbeats and Cyrus' laboured breathing. It was during one of these silences that I saw his tired, yellow eyes roll over toward me, and then to my mother. She knew what he was saying to her, and she turned to me with a remote look of pleasure.

"Maury, he'd like you to change your name to Wick," she said quietly.

I stared at her, thoroughly shocked, motionless. It had never occurred to me, after more than a decade of imposed discrimination, that the old man would ever invite me to take his family's name. It had rarely occurred to me even as a child to long for this — and now, as he was fading into eternity, he was extending this strange and unexpected offer.

Of course he had not expressed it himself, not verbally, not to me. There could never be that. Cyrus had never learned what it felt like to talk directly to me in the way adult human beings converse under normal circumstances. Even in this final gallant gesture, he could not muster up the civility to suit the occasion. Instead, he had talked to my mother, the eternal go-between, and she relayed the precious invitation in his presence.

By now, however, I was beyond malice. I had no cynical reply to offer, no angry floodtide of resentment to pour out on him. He had wrung all of that awful potential out of me years before, through a diet of sheer intimidation.

I could not respond to the statement, as Mum and Cyrus looked at me for an answer. What a sea change, to take the name Maury Wick after seventeen years as Maury Blair! I felt no forced distance between myself and the name, no cringing at the thought because of everything it symbolized. Those feelings had been razed and scraped away over the long years. Now I felt only an odd sense of alienation, as if too much had happened to Maury Blair for him to suddenly shed the name and take on another — any other.

It was perhaps the final abuse. Cyrus could no longer hit me, and with my place as the oldest resident child he could no longer ignore me. So he would strip me of the one possession I had managed to hang onto for myself: my identity.

I thanked him politely for making the offer. But I could make no commitment. I was unwilling to part with my name;

it was the only thing in life I could consider truly mine. And Mum graciously changed the subject.

The end was inevitable. During the final hours, after the doctors had shaken their heads with grim hopelessness and left the room for the last time, I sat on a wooden chair outside the door, alone in the corridor, listening to the awful sounds of death conquering life. The lion was dying.

I heard him crying "Oh, God!" in virtual delirium, and although I had no relationship with the Almighty, I prayed nevertheless that the old man would make his peace with God. If there was any redemption available in eternity for a life so ill-spent, I wanted him in those moments to have access to it. No more suffering for suffering's sake.

When the nurse came out and reported that he had died, I stood up and walked in to the foot of the bed. He lay there silent, still, as he had for days, his mustache tinted by nicotine in exactly the same brown yellow as the first and second fingers of his right hand. The wretchedness had ended. The furious monster, so terrible in life, lay awkward and pitiable in death, the life sucked out of him by some greater, even more terrible force.

The next day I was summoned back to the hospital to pick up his hat and coat. It was difficult for me to maintain composure as I carried the empty garments down the corridor and out of the building. He had vanished. All that toughness had finally been forced to submit. Viewing this wasted end of a wasted life, I felt a droopy sadness in my heart.

At the funeral, I watched the parade pass by, each participant dutifully shaking my hand and noting by the momentary gleam in his eye that, ah yes, I was the odd one, the one he had hated. Lud and Selma were there, from the terrible far years before. They acknowledged no earlier problems, only went through the usual funereal motions. Others came, said their expected pieces, did their duty.

It was an Anglican funeral, according to Cyrus' long-lost heritage, performed in the funeral home with the proper portions of solemnity and positive thinking. But I heard little of the minister's packaged sermon. I looked at the casket, at the stiff profile of the man who had brought such chaos to my early life, and I realized what it was about Cyrus Wick that had redeemed him to me. He lay there motionless, a brick of lifeless flesh, and by his very stillness he revealed to me the quality that I had come to rely on in him.

He was always there.

In a perverse way, he had become a source of security for me. He inspired fear, even panic, he turned my intestines into cramping knots, he destroyed year after formative year of my life, and yet he was always there. He had always been there, a hub, a source of sameness. Mum had come and gone, leaving home for weeks at a time, flighty and irresponsible and guilt-ridden at various junctures. The siblings had drifted away with the years. Only Cyrus remained.

It was a sameness I required, a stability that my warped inner being had to have if I was to hold on and survive into adulthood. Now, though, as the shell of the old man lay cushioned in white satin, I realized that the rock had finally been crushed. The cornerstone of security, no matter how tenuous or destructive, had always been there in my life — until now.

And I would have to find that foundation of security, that hope, that consistency, somewhere else.

Mum was stunned by the loss, even though it had been expected for so long, and even though it had to bring at least a measure of relief to her. Her instincts told her, once again, to flee.

I hated the idea of leaving Paris, particularly just now with the minor upheaval caused by Cyrus' death, and my work solidly established in the textile mill, and life just on the verge of finally evening out. But she insisted, nervous and troubled and ill at ease. She wanted to run, to get out, to move.

A succession of unhappy moves blackened the following months. Initially we stored our worn furniture in Rose's basement and headed for Flint. One of Mom's sisters who lived there thought she could get Mum a job in the department store where she worked. Once they were both on the inside, they began trying to find a position for me. But I sat at home for weeks, waiting, bored and restless and cranky.

Finally I was able to take a spot in the store's shipping department. As a Canadian-born alien without a work permit, I reverted to Mum's old lie and told the personnel office I had been born in Ohio. When an American team trounced a Canadian team and my co-workers sneered among themselves at the "stupid Canucks," I had to bite my tongue.

But it was boring work, and I longed to return to grimy Paris. I was glad when Mum changed her mind about the qualities of Flint, Michigan, and decided she wanted to go back to Canada. We heard there were jobs in Hamilton, Ontario, but got there and discovered otherwise within a few months. Finally we completed the circle and tramped back into Paris, where we moved into the upstairs of a friend's house until we could locate a place of our own.

Mum knew a man in town who rented houses. The only one he had available at the time had been condemned by health officials, but he agreed to let us stay there on the sly for a couple weeks, until something else opened up.

Something else never opened up. The hovel became our home.

It was the small, ugly house sandwiched between two big nice houses, the one you were embarrassed to be seen going into. We knew some of the neighbours in the area, which made matters even less pleasant. Our rent was shamefully low, but it was a burden even so. We were living on unemployment insurance. It seemed as if there were no jobs available for us anywhere on the continent.

The house was flimsy, poorly built to the extreme that health officials had decreed that no one should live in it until major repairs had been done on it. The owner didn't have the money to spend on renovation. Slats in the walls had shrunk and warped and the wind whistled through them unabated. The plaster had cracked completely away in the upstairs rooms, revealing industrious mother birds feeding their young in cozy wall-nests.

But I had gravitated into position as the head of the house, and I had a will to work. The environment was no longer totally out of my control, and I took to improving it with vigor. My younger brothers and I knocked out a wall to enlarge the cramped living room, repaired other walls, and repainted the dreary exterior.

Still, I was nineteen years old, and without a future. I was dogged by a vague, persistent loneliness, an inner hunger that refused to be fed. I stretched out in my bed beside the solitary lamp and spent endless hours reading pointless books and twisting the tuning dial on my dusty radio. I liked rock music, and sometimes jazz, but I constantly found myself tuning out the ubiquitous Billy Graham, who invariably interrupted my listening, especially on Sunday evenings, with his disgusting *Hour of Decision*.

A friend of my mother passed along a book, and Mum by her custom passed it along to me. It was all about positive thinking, that sort of thing, and the friend thought it would help down-trodden Alice. Mum skimmed through it casually and likewise thought it might give me a boost.

Then came the explosion.

CHAPTER NINE
Chain Reaction

For God so loved the world,
that He gave His only begotten Son,
that whosoever believeth in Him should not perish,
but have everlasting life.

— John 3:16

CHAPTER NINE
Chain Reaction

It was just another book, really, in a long line of books consumed in boredom under the flat yellow light of my bedroom lamp. I thumbed my way into it with the same lackluster diffidence that I had begun the reading of dozens of others.

There was no crisis in my life at the moment to generate some special interest, some anxious searching for The Answer in the pages of this book more than any other book. My entire life had been a crisis, and no book — nor person, nor institution, nor philosophy — had ever brought resolution. I was a shrugging victim of life's erratic hard knocks. Indeed, I set the book aside for several days, often looking over there at it, but always deciding consciously not to pick it up and start on it.

Perhaps it was this weird calm, the lack of any panic or disaster, that greased my spiritual chute and drew me in. Whatever the reason, I was to realize later, I was primed to absorb what I read in those still, quiet evening hours as I sprawled across the bed.

As the words and sentences and paragraphs rolled by, I discovered movement: I was going somewhere, through this book, that I had never been before. I was reading Scriptures on these pages, quotations from the Bible in a context of sensible, uplifting, reasonable English.

And it was all saying one thing to me: God loved me.

"That's it!" I said to myself. "That's what I've been looking for!" God loved me!

Every time the concept leaped off the page again, I

experienced the warm rush of revelation, of fresh and happy realization, and of gratefulness. God loved me! The God I had heard about, the one I had learned to pray to by rote in Gospel Cadets as a child, the one I had begged help from during those cold nights outside the house — that God loved me.

It was such a novel thought that I turned it over and over and over again in my head, as if it were a huge glorious shining red apple to be inspected and marveled at for long, delicious minutes before the ecstatic eating of it should begin. God loved me. The wet rat, trapped for years in a place where he wasn't wanted, the animal, forced to make his own way on the streets, eating outside, or upstairs, or not at all — God loved that animal. The child of woe, born in tragic passion, reared in passionate tragedy — God loved that woeful child. God loved me.

If anyone had been watching me as the transformation began, they would have detected little in the way of physical change. A shifting on the bed, an unplanned flexing of the leg muscles, perhaps, but nothing more. I said no word, but inside I was stretching to take in this strange and fantastic new spiritual food. Amazing — that the supreme God, Creator of the Universe, loved me!

I did not understand what was happening to me. The closest I had ever come to true love was wanting to be wanted — and there was little comparison! Now, even in my struggling ignorance, without being able to comprehend the experience I was having, I knew I wanted more, and I knew I wanted it to last — like a baby bird stretching wide his beak for Mother's food.

No one had talked to me. I wouldn't have understood that jargon anyway. The clichés in the book were meaningless to me; all I could glean was the revolutionizing fact that God loved me, that He knew me personally and wanted to have a personal relationship with me, wanted to be my friend and protector. I heard no sermons, listened to no gospel music — I was simply saved.

My mother detected the change in me instantly. My face, once grim and clouded, was clear now. There was a light in my eyes, a little beaming that would grow and grow as the days progressed. I told her about the impact I had felt the night before as I read the book, and her face reacted with a restrained but very real joy — she perhaps held back, having grown accustomed to bad news instead of good, and disappointment on the heels of happiness.

I paced to the local library, determined to find more of this. The religious section had never existed for me before — I had rarely ever been inside a library in the first place — but now it was a bustling marketplace where the stunning current of spiritual power could be accessed again. The lending limit was four books, so I found four with promise and walked to the check-out counter. The librarian knew me. She looked at the book covers and then up at me, a blank expression on her face.

"These are religious books," she said in a tone that matched her face.

"Yes," I said with equal evenness.

"You're taking them out?" she asked, her eyes reflecting a very subdued version of shock.

"Yes."

She looked back down at the books and paused only another moment. "Okay," she finally said, and began stamping the return dates inside each of them.

The return dates were unnecessary. I lay awake the entire night, never lapsing into fatigue, only more and more energized by the amazing twist my life had so suddenly taken. Page after page, chapter after chapter, through all four books I pored. From my personal starting line, with virtually no knowledge of God's personality and character, I was sprinting forward, tearing up the track, to learn everything, as much as a man could in a single night's reading. Every new revelation lifted me to a new plane of refreshing satisfaction, and yet I was far from being satisfied. Charging forward through the black hours of the earliest morning, I filled myself with the delight of knowing a personal God, and then filled myself some more, and some more, and yet more.

The next evening I faced the librarian once again, the same four books in hand and ready to be turned over.

"You didn't like them?" she asked, her face implying the added "I told you so."

"I enjoyed them very much," I replied with a smile.

She was startled. "When did you read them?"

"Last night."

"All of them?"

"Yes," I nodded, grinning at her.

I left the counter, with the librarian standing mildly stupefied over the four books, and began the search for my next four acquisitions.

Night after night the scene was the same in my room: the lamp, the books, the starving child gobbling up newfound goodies. My mother, increasingly pleased to see the wonderful addiction taking such deep hold, encouraged me to keep reading. When I grew frustrated reading quoted Scripture passages in my books and not owning a Bible of my own, she dug out her dead mother's old Bible, one of the earliest looseleaf editions ever printed, and turned it over to me for study. It was full of Grandma's ancient notes and my mother's notations from her days as an evangelist.

The Bible was an even newer beginning, as I began to see in the Word things that had been happening to me — experiences of my own, confirmed in Scriptures. "If any man be in Christ," I read in the apostle Paul's letter to the Corinthians, "he is a new creature. Behold, all things are become new!"

I read about Christ's encounter with Nicodemus in John's gospel, and realized that I had been born again, having accepted God's love for me through the sacrifice of His Son. It was a beautiful dawning for me.

Billy Graham's once-obnoxious *Hour of Decision* became my media ministry. I twisted the dials persistently, trying to tune in those programs that I had once irritably avoided.

And the voracious reading continued. I slumped in my bed upstairs and smoked cigarettes and read books about Jesus. I sat at the kitchen table downstairs with a cup of coffee and smoked cigarettes and read books about Jesus. Wherever I could find a reasonable amount of quiet, whenever I could set aside the minutiae of everyday life that now seemed so inconsequential, I put myself in front of another page of Scripture, and began drinking it in.

The revealing of God's love for me continued to overwhelm

me. It did not grow stale or cold with time. In wave after wave, I felt the continual renewing of His life within me, as I saw and then affirmed and then re-affirmed that He saw me in all my weaknesses and faults and flaws and still accepted me — unattractive, unwanted, unclean. And indeed, He loved me.

By the hour, I studied and prayed, seeking deep communion with my Lord. When I had absorbed as much reading as I could handle in a sitting, I walked a couple doors down to the river and leaned on the fence. Overlooking the water as the sun dipped out of view, I thought through the truths I had read, and about what was happening inside of me, meditating on the bigness and the goodness and the compassion of the Heavenly Father. I didn't want to be around people for a while, I just wanted to be with my Father, alone with Him, to learn more about Him after so many years of isolation from Him. I wanted to find His heart, to go wherever it was. For weeks and months I lived in the glow of that new relationship, the new sonship I had discovered.

And God demonstrated His love and omnipotence to me in graphic ways. As money continued to dry up, our fuel supply dwindled. When we finally had only enough wood to activate the central stove in the house, we all gathered around it for the wintry night. I prayed that God would provide. The next morning a local man dropped by to ask a favour. Would we test a season's worth of green wood for him and let him know if it was a good product before he purchased a larger quantity from his supplier? Supercharged with the confirmation of God's loving power, I began unloading the huge mass of wood from his wagon.

But I had much to learn, even after weeks and months of concentrated study and prayer and basking in the light. I had not yet discovered the strength that comes from human relationships within the Body of Christ. I had not yet learned the importance of fellowship, of intercessory prayer, of learning from those whom God anoints as teachers and leaders. I had no understanding of worship in the corporate sense, no inkling as to the inter-relationship of Christian people.

All of which made my first setback all the more painful

and lonely.

I was taking a walk on a Sunday evening, ambling toward the downtown area of Paris, slouching into depression. Satan was feeding me his side of the story. I was scarred up inside, with a lifetime of sorrow written on my heart. I was ensnared by habits, and I saw myself as a rotten specimen. As I allowed my mind to work me over, I had come to see myself as too befouled to have any worth in God's family. There was the ugliness of illegitimacy, which I had eventually come to see plainly, in spite of my mother's mismatched stories. There were the years of sin, years of ignoring the persistent impulses of conscience that I now recognized as the work of God's Holy Spirit. There was so much sheer background to deal with, and I was struggling with the weight of it.

Unable to release the burden, and unwilling to weep openly, I stood on a street corner downtown and looked up in the general direction of the place I imagined Him to be.

"God, take my name out of your book," I said flatly. "I can't hack it any longer. Just wipe me out."

I did not want to leave God behind. I did not want anything but the new life, full of love, that I had experienced with such a luxurious satisfaction over the past several months. But I was convinced by Satan's insistent accusations: I had no choice; I was not good enough for God, and I would never be. It was too late.

With an under-developed understanding of God's character, I thought the party was over. I thought I would walk on, end up in my room, and return to the drab life I had known — because God would follow my instructions. My heart ached, but I muscled up my emotions and determined to survive the loss, just as I had survived everything else in my life.

I threw myself carelessly across the bed and reached for the radio dial. Back to the old rock and roll, I figured, to drown out my sorrow in the beating of drums.

But my Father had claimed me. I was no more out of His sight or mind than Billy Graham himself. As I turned on the radio, the *Hour of Decision* was just coming on over the air, with the choir ringing out "How Great Thou Art." I was gripped by the sound, and I lay still, not dialing it out, but drinking it in.

After the music, Graham stepped to his microphone and began preaching. Every word clung to me. "You don't just walk away from God," he said over and over. And as he talked, I could almost see my Heavenly Father feeling the same sorrow of rejection that I had once felt. I could almost see Him weeping as I walked away from Him on that downtown street corner. But He hadn't just stood still, He hadn't just walked the other way. He had followed me. He had been following me along. His infinite love for me would not let me escape. He loved me too much to let me go. His mere sorrow, my mere depression, would not stand in His way. My Father loved me as His son. I was His.

I clutched my pillow to my face and began crying out loud to God, begging His forgiveness, pleading temporary insanity for the instructions I had given Him on that street corner.

"I didn't mean it," I cried again and again. "Don't wipe my name out of the book."

For three hours I prayed continuously, until finally I felt the certainty of real peace, until I knew without any doubt that Christ had committed Himself to me even more surely than I had committed myself to Him. When I realized that He had not given up on me, even though I tried to give up on Him, my entire outlook changed. I began to live and operate with that sure-fire strength of commitment: Jesus doesn't just pick up and leave. He stays. He stays when everyone else has left. He stays when even you have left! Eternity is His only calendar. He doesn't desert you from one day to the next.

It was the blossoming for me. I never looked back. Finally I had found an eternal source of fuel for life: the love of a Heavenly Father. Mum loved me, but she had not always been there. Cyrus had always been there, but he never loved me. I had never known anything like what I was experiencing now, but what I was experiencing now had me reeling with joy. The old person in me fell away, the habits and insecurities shed like old sunburn.

A locomotive chain reaction had already begun. We began going to the nearby Pentecostal Sunday school each weekend. It was a bit frightening for me at first — I thought everyone would turn around to stare at Maury Blair and say, "What's *he* doing here?" But the first Sunday morning, as we sat waiting for class to begin, I felt a friendly hand on my shoulder. Turning around I saw the pastor, Jack Ozard, smiling down at me.

"Hi, how are you doing?" he asked.

"Fine, thanks," I responded stiffly.

"We've got a youth class upstairs. Would you like to join us? We'd be glad to have you."

I was too startled by the friendly offer to accept it.

"No, thanks, I'll stay here."

"Are you sure?" he asked, still smiling easily. "We'd love to have you join us."

"No, thanks."

I turned around in my chair, wishing I had responded differently.

Eventually, Jack's warm openness drew me in, and I ended up sitting under his great personal ministry in a class with other young people about my age. Eventually Jack would become my most valued counselor and friend.

My enthusiasm spread throughout our house, and my brothers and sisters began attending the Sunday school along with Mum and me. Finally I worked up the nerve to ask Jack if it would be all right for us to attend a service on a Sunday night.

He was astounded by the question.

"All right?" he replied. "We'd be delighted to have you there!"

I was surprised that there was no hesitation, no pause to consider the ramifications of inviting "those Wicks" to a worship service in that reputable church. But no — Jack opened his arms wide to us, and the whole family was swept in by the love of the pastor and his people.

Week after week I drank in the precious new wine, feeding on the teaching of Scripture and the fellowship of believers that I had never known. As I strived to live life according to what I was learning, I found I needed more from God, and I prayed to be baptized in the Holy Spirit. It was a beautiful, quiet experience, alone in my room at home, that turned yet another spiritual corner for me and gave me a burst of renewed hope and energy as a Christian.

God provided other helps in my earliest days as a believer. I landed a job at the Wincey Mills and discovered that my superintendent, John Richardson, was a Christian brother. My brother Mark had already worked under John and had established a terrible reputation. John hired me on a gamble, before either of us knew the other was a Christian. When we saw each other in church the following Sunday morning, it was the beginning of a wonderful friendship.

As each of my other brothers came back home periodically, they were stunned by the change that had so obviously occurred. I had begun praying fervently for Mark and Frank especially, certain that if God could save them He could save anybody. Mark was in the navy, living a godless, rowdy life. He came home on leave and was disgusted to learn that we were praying for him. One evening as I sat at the kitchen table reading my Bible, he sat down across from me with the bottle of liquor and proceeded to ridicule me and all of Christianity as he drank the entire bottle. When he ran out of liquor, he stood up to get more and promptly passed out. I helped him up to bed, and the next morning he came downstairs for breakfast to find me once again reading my Bible. The hunt was on; God would not let go of Mark.

Dogged by the convicting power of the Holy Spirit, Mark performed erratically when he returned to navy duty. Soon he was under the analysis of a navy psychiatrist. After a few sessions the doctor declared, "Wick, there's something you are not doing that you need to do, and whatever it is, you better do it."

Mark came home for the Christmas holidays. His New Year's Eve plan was to take an old girl friend out on the town. She was unhappily married and Mark intended to redeem her holiday. Mum and I started in on him, along with the younger brothers and sisters, pressuring him mercilessly to cancel his date and join us for the traditional watchnight service at our church. Resist as he might, he finally caved in.

The presence of the Lord filled the sanctuary in a mighty way, and Mark had no resistance left. He gave his heart and life unconditionally to Jesus Christ that evening, and began living a vibrant, exuberant brand of Christianity from that moment on.

Frank, meanwhile, had been living in Michigan. When he visited us in Paris, we persuaded him to attend a rally at the Pentecostal Braeside Camp outside town, the same campgrounds I had cruised years earlier with my buddies, haranguing the Christians. It was a powerful service, with a riveting sermon by the guest evangelist. At its conclusion, as the preacher invited sinners to give their lives to Christ at the altars, Frank stood and dashed toward him. For one terrified moment I thought he was going to give the evangelist a furious beating, but as Frank approached the front, he fell to his knees and began weeping. God miraculously changed Frank's life in those intense moments.

Each of the other brothers and sisters would have their own personal "hours of decision" as the loving touch of the Heavenly Father redeemed and restored the lost years.

Mum was thrilled. She realized that in spite of her own weaknesses, God had reached down and touched her family.

There were times of testing. In my first experience as a street witness, distributing gospel tracts to passersby in downtown Paris, some of my old friends came by and spat on me to express the depths of their contempt. But day by day, God ministered growth and redemption to a life that had known only stagnation and loss. I eventually took on the teaching of a Sunday school class, leadership of the church's Crusaders program for young boys, and membership on the board of deacons. Still I couldn't get enough of the Lord, enough of the Word, and I enrolled in a correspondence course to discover still more of this fascinating new life.

My frenetic routine started at five every morning, when I rose to begin my studies for the day. From seven to five I worked at the mill, then came home for a quick supper. If I could, I napped till eight-thirty. Then it was back to the studies, usually until one in the morning. After four hours of sleep, the agenda began all over again, with me fantasizing about becoming the Twentieth Century Apostle Paul and sailing across the ocean to launch a fabulous missionary operation.

I was a long way from my childhood, and further yet from

the man who had fathered me — the original Maury Blair. But I would face him one day.

CHAPTER TEN
"You Don't Exist"

> The least initial deviation from the
> truth is multiplied later a thousand-fold.
>
> — *Aristotle, circa 375 B.C.*

CHAPTER TEN
"You Don't Exist"

My high-powered pace of work and study soon caught up with me, and I ended up sitting in a doctor's office, exhausted. The doctor quizzed me about my lifestyle, and the source of my fatigue soon became evident. I had been considering a missionary position in the hot West Indies, but he ruled it out for me. The heat would destroy me in my weakened condition, he insisted. I had been offered the pastorate of a small church, but I felt uncomfortable with the idea of pastoring, especially as a single person. And I had no desire to marry; I had seen quite enough of the pitfalls marriage could hold.

But then there was the option of going to Bible college for a year, to relax and study.

"That's it!" the doctor said, snapping his fingers. "It will be perfect for you. Take my advice. I'm an old man and you're a young man. Slow down!"

I left his office wondering what a doctor could know about spiritual things. I would get my direction from God, I told myself, not some doctor. For the next few days I petitioned God desperately: what did He want of me? On Sunday afternoon, as I prayed sitting on the edge of my bed, I heard a voice.

"You're going to Bible school." the voice said, and I heard a book close with a loud slap.

Instantly I fell asleep. In an hour I awoke, and the anxiety of the decision had fled. I was at complete peace, and I began planning for Bible school.

The year at Eastern Pentecostal Bible College in Peterborough, Ontario, was a recuperative and refreshing one. My studies drew me deeper yet into the Word. At the same time, my dorm-mates and I found our way into constant college mischief, springing friendly practical jokes on faculty and students alike with tantalizing unpredictability. My closest friends — Dave Distaulo, Ed Morrison, and Doug Hagey — determined to marry me off and secretly organized a "Maury Blair Day," on which they peppered the entire campus with billboards declaring my availability for courtship. Between water fights and clothing theft and assorted other campus clownings, the long-hidden Maury Blair emerged. With the shell of loneliness and insecurity finally broken, I found a comfortable fun-loving Maury inside.

All of which would be required for my first task after college, as a counselor at the Teen Haven residential ministry for young people in Montreal, Quebec, under the leadership of Pastor Robert Johnston. Here, teenagers who had squandered themselves on drugs or alcohol were housed and cared for and led into the love of the Lord. It was often tense, erratic, disturbing work — and without the flexibility I had acquired at school, I might never have survived.

As it turned out, it was at Teen Haven that God began revealing to me how my childhood, horrible as it was, could be used by Him as a vessel of ministry to others. I noticed a young boy lazing around the Teen Haven center one day, looking despondent and directionless.

"What's the matter, Jake?" I asked, sitting down next to him.

He sighed heavily, "Aw, *you* wouldn't know anything about hiding and being on the run," he replied.

I felt a flood of empathy for him as I heard his words. In the next few minutes, I told him some of my story. He looked at me in amazement, seeing not the rat-like child I described, but a re-constituted child of God. It was the beginning of a new life for Jake — and for me.

Since that encounter, I have had countless opportunities to share parts of my past with young people in trouble, young people who feel, as I did, that God could certainly never want them since no people had ever wanted them. Again and again, I've seen the beautiful wellspring of revelation in the faces of troubled teenagers as they begin to sense the endless love of a

106

Heavenly Father, a Father who has been there all along, just asking for their love.

It was during my work at Teen Haven that I met Bev. For the first time in my life, I considered leaving bachelorhood. I was already past thirty, well on my way to fulfilling my dream of emulating the Apostle Paul's singlehood, when Bev's big brown eyes and exuberant personality broke my stride.

She was the product of a Christian home, a godly young lady, and great fun. I loved to be with her. When I was with her, I was caught up. When I was away from her, my mind floated back to her over and over.

But there was something about me, something she should know. I could not know how she would react, but I knew I could never afford to let her find out some other way.

"I need to tell you something," I offered tentatively on a foggy Saturday evening as we walked together. I meandered through my reasons for being at Teen Haven, my hopes for ministering to young people, and finally I came down to my own youth.

"I had some problems as a young person," I said in a hopefully casual tone. "I was a bastard child."

Bev looked at me with a question in her eyes. Her own heritage, which was very proper and somewhat sheltered, had not included such a concept, and it was a foreign term to her.

"What do you mean?" she asked.

I explained as delicately as I could, all the while watching her face to see if the new insight would drive her off.

"I'm so sorry for you," she replied evenly, unsure about the proper response. But inside, her heart was swelling with compassion. God had already begun dealing with her. *It would be wonderful,* she prayed silently, *if I could make a home for him, if I could show him another side of life.*

Before it could happen, though, Bev would have to be exposed to more of the old side of life.

Mum was happy for me when I told her I was going to be married. Several of my brothers and sisters met in Cambridge, Ontario, for a makeshift reunion, and in that setting Bev and my mother were introduced. It was a polite encounter, with only the ill unease that people customarily feel when they meet relatives-to-be.

It was the birth certificate problem that opened old wounds. Bev offered to apply for our marriage license; all I had to do was give her my birth certificate.

"I don't have one," I had to answer. I had learned it years before, but I had studiously avoided discussing the subject with anyone.

"Everybody has a birth certificate," Bev replied. "Just write away for it."

But my mother had failed to register me, and there was no document to write for.

I would have to confront my mother.

"I know I wasn't registered," I began quietly, and I could see her face droop with sadness. "But I need a birth certificate to get married, Mum. What do I have to do to get one?"

She took a long breath and let it escape slowly. Her past, so often swept under the emotional carpet, had billowed up like a dust cloud once again.

"We could go to the registrar's office and check on it," she said, looking at the floor.

Perhaps she foresaw the ordeal it would be.

The registrar was a gruff, older man. As we sat down across the desk from him, he dispensed with the simple questions quickly — name, age, address — and bore in to the tough material.

"Why wasn't he registered when he was born?" he demanded of her.

"Well, he was born in a house," Mum answered haltingly, "and born out of wedlock."

"That's no reason for not registering him," the man growled. Then he turned to me. "Have you ever signed any legal documents?"

"Well, I guess I have. Why?"

"It's illegal," he snapped, "because you're not registered."

My mind flew through the list of documents I had signed — mortgage papers, auto financing, and a dozen others.

"You don't even belong here," the man continued. "You're presently the citizen of no country. You don't belong here, you don't belong anywhere."

Mum was crushed. The registrar was feeding on her obvious sense of guilt, making her suffer all over again for sins long past.

"For all intents and purposes," he went on, "you don't exist. How do I know this woman is your mother? How can she prove you're her son?"

My mother sat humiliated, and I was angry.

"Listen, Mack," I shot back at the man, "this happens to be my mother. And if anybody should be mad at her, it should be me — not you. So please treat her with respect."

The man backed down, surprised by the reprimand. We proceeded to work out a system for getting him some shred of documentation as to my existence — Mum suggested my stay at the London hospital as an infant, which I had never known about. When those records arrived at the registrar's office, the birth certificate was generated and sent to me. Finally, I existed.

And yet more of my past would be dredged up.

Bev and I worked together as husband and wife with increasing enthusiasm, first at Teen Haven, later in a church in Hanover, Ontario, then at the Teen Challenge center for youth rehabilitation in Toronto. Bev was my "second revolution," the perfect partner to help me grow spiritually and emotionally after the amazing "first revolution" of salvation and redemption. Her loving touch transformed me once again, giving me that full swell of God's best, as she worked alongside me day by day.

In Toronto, Lisa was born, and I wept as I looked at the tiny newborn baby. It was the first time Bev had ever seen me cry, but the flood of emotion was too much to hold back. This infant was mine — ours — and God's.

Looking at the tiny kicking legs and flailing arms, the little round face so full of hope, I realized in a new way how gracious God is. I had been born in the squalor of hushed scandal; God had allowed me to give my own child a transformed heritage. A few years later, after our ministry had carried us to Vancouver,

British Columbia, Laury would follow Lisa into the new, brighter world God had given us.

In the Vancouver Teen Challenge center, and eventually as the director of the Toronto Teen Challenge ministry, I found that God was taking me through crises in the lives of others that brought my own dreary childhood into a new perspective. As I ministered with my staff members at rock festivals and in alleyways, on street corners and in crashpads, I found young people all over the nation of Canada whose lives were tailspinning. And the tragedies were all the more poignant because in so many cases these teenagers had abused themselves. They had not needed a Cyrus Wick. Many had enjoyed the parentage of Christian people. And yet they had literally taken themselves apart piece by piece, some by drug abuse, some by alcoholism, others by a variety of excesses.

Again and again the gruesome experiences of my past bore fruit in the re-telling. A young man named Phil came to the Toronto center one day and told me his two brothers were just about to crash and burn if they didn't get help soon. They were holed up with some friends, feeding on acid and speed, in a crashpad near our center, and he wanted me to pay them a visit with him right away. I agreed.

"Just let me warn you before we go," Phil added. "Sometimes their friends get high on LSD. I've seen them running through the house with machetes, doing all kinds of crazy things."

The big red light went on inside me.

"Now just a minute," I said to Phil, "let's talk about this whole thing."

"Don't worry about it," he assured me. "If I go in there, I can handle them. I have a pretty good influence on them. They'll listen to me. I can get you in there to talk to these guys, and they won't do anything to you, I promise."

With plenty of reservations about it, I agreed to go.

"You can't go like that," Phil said, as if he were startled that I would even consider it.

"What do you mean?" I asked.

"They'll think you're a cop if you go in like that," he

responded directly. I was wearing a sports jacket and slacks. "You'll have to change."

I changed into blue jeans, scooped some gospel literature into my briefcase, and we took off.

On the way to the pad, Phil unloaded his story. He was a blackslidden Christian. He had come to Teen Challenge for help because he knew that the Lord was the only hope his kid brothers had. When I told him my own story briefly, he reacted with enthusiasm.

"That's what these guys need to hear," he said emphatically. "You've got to tell them that."

We pulled the car up in front of a grubby old house. A couple doors down, I noticed, was a house with several motorcycles parked on the front lawn.

"I'd take you in there, too," Phil said. "There's a guy in there dying of drug abuse. But they'd kill you as you walked in the front door, so I can't take you in there."

I breathed a silent sigh of relief. One crashpad in a day was more than enough for me.

"Just a minute," I said, stopping Phil at the door. "Before we go in, we're going to pray."

"Pray?"

"Pray."

"Are you scared?"

"Yes."

"Oh."

"We're going to pray and ask God to help us say the right things when we get in there." I bowed my head and prayed quickly, both for Phil to renew his commitment to the Lord, and for his burned-out brothers inside.

As he opened the door, the sweltering summer heat and the stench of pot and urine blasted us. We made our way through the house, stepping over intertwined bodies and around wobbling tokers, until we came to the long narrow kitchen. I instinctively glanced around the room for possible escape routes. I had already come through too much house to get back out that way. The back door was at the opposite end of the kitchen, past the two guys sitting on chairs along the wall, past the big guy with the red beard standing solemnly in front of the door, past the four others sitting around the kitchen table rolling joints. There was only one window: it was high on the wall, almost to the ceiling, and too small for an adult to climb through under the best of circumstances, which these were not. I was trapped. I would get out of this place with the approval of my hosts, or I would not get out at all.

Phil and I stood next to the grimy refrigerator, and Phil addressed the rag-tag group.

"All right, you guys, listen. This guy's name is Maury Blair. He's a friend of mine, and I want you to shut up and listen to what he's got to say, because I think you need to hear it."

Then Phil turned and walked out of the room.

I never saw him or heard from him again — ever.

I was too startled at his abrupt exit to stop him. Instead, as I realized that the entire kitchen full of people was staring at me, I spoke up, trying to sound unworried.

"Hi, guys," I began. "I'm Maury Blair, and I'm a staff worker from Teen Challenge on Broadview Avenue."

It was the worst thing I could have said. The big guy with the red beard standing at the doorway spoke.

"Teen Challenge?" he drawled. "You guys kicked me out of there a couple months ago."

My heart began pounding even faster. "I don't know anything about that," I assured him, "but I'm here to tell you that there's a better trip for you than the one you're on."

If these guys go bananas, I'm dead, I said to myself. Suddenly, going out in a blaze of glory like the Apostle Paul didn't hold the old glamour for me.

"I don't know why you got kicked out of Teen Challenge," I pressed on, "but I do know that God loves you guys and wants to change your lives. He did it for me, and He wants to do it for you."

"What's God going to do for me, man?" the red-bearded guy sneered. "I've got a disease in my liver from sticking dirty needles in my arms. I've got nine months to live. What's God going to do for me?"

"Maybe God could just touch your life and heal you," I suggested boldly.

"What about my kid brother here?" he asked, pointing to his right. "He's got the same problem. What about him?"

Suddenly I realized that these were the two brothers Phil had brought me to see. The whole picture fell together in that moment.

"God could do the same for him," I responded.

I began to share my story with the group, telling them how God had rescued me from the seemingly impossible. When I had finished, I said, "Look, you guys, here's the truth. I didn't have to come here tonight. I'm at your mercy. I came because I knew God wanted me to. Phil told me what was going on here, but I'm not the heat. I'm here taking all the risks to tell you God can change your life."

"Hey, you know something? He's right," one of the group said. "He didn't have to come."

With the ice broken, the various people began talking, asking questions about my past, about my faith, and allowing me to share Jesus with them.

In moments I felt like the best friend these guys had ever had. They eagerly took every piece of literature I had brought with me. They slapped me on the back, shook my hand, smiled. A minister who cared about them — it was novel for them.

Two hours after I arrived, I left the place, swimming in my own sweat, exhausted from the tension of the experience. Only God could have given me the words, in answer to my frightened prayer, that opened the doors and allowed me to minister freely. The tragic experiences, re-lived in this grotesque setting, had borne fruit once again.

Three weeks later I returned to the center from a speaking engagement to find a message. Two young men had visited the center and asked to see me. The message they left: "Tell Maury Blair that we dropped by to say thanks for having the guts to come up to us and tell us what God did for him. We're brothers, and we're going home to Hamilton with our parents, and we're going to stay there where we belong. Just tell him thanks."

As my ministry unfolded, my history likewise unfolded.

d

CHAPTER ELEVEN
Fathers

Before I formed thee
in the belly I knew thee;
and before thou camest
forth out of the womb
I sanctified thee...

— Jeremiah 1:5

CHAPTER ELEVEN
Fathers

Before my mother died of cancer, a thin-haired and fragile shadow of the beauty she once had been, she inexplicably opened up to Bev over tea one afternoon. As she talked, she unraveled many of the mysteries that had bound up my past for years. She talked about my biological father, how she felt about him, how she fled the factory when she learned she was pregnant. Some of the details, difficult to swallow, are not confirmable. Their veracity will never be known.

Mum, at the end, was an apologetic, defeated woman. She had given her life back to the Lord years before, she had moved into a cottage on the campgrounds at Braeside, she had encouraged her children in their various ministries; but she never entirely out-distanced her guilt. "Maury, I've made such a mess of my life," she whimpered so often when I talked with her privately. I drove home the message of forgiveness again and again to her, reminding her how "the blood of Jesus cleanseth from all sin." But to no avail. She could never stop fleeing entirely. She ran from her past until she died.

It was only after the funeral, as I stood at the grave and watched the coffin lowered into the earth, that I felt a particular freedom — the freedom to search for my biological father. Bev had encouraged me in it, and my interest in the mission grew over the years. But I knew what deep hurts it could cause among the members of my family, and for Mum especially, so I had moved very slowly and carefully.

I had never felt anger toward the mystery man whose chromosomes I carried in my body. I had known too little of him, I had been introduced to him through too complicated a maze of untruths and half-truths over too great a span of time. At no intersection of my life did I ever get a full report or comprehensive description of the original Maury Blair. Was he a war hero? It became clear years later that he was not, although he may have had a military background that gave impetus to my mother's farfetched lie. Did he die in the World War? That we eventually determined to be untrue altogether. Who visited the London hospital during my stay there as an infant and signed in as Maury Blair? Had the original Maury Blair surfaced for some unknown reason? Or was it someone else, using a name my mother had supplied? My mother never provided an answer. The answer can probably never be known.

Bev and I began to pursue the mystery father even before Mum died, and Bev's artful questioning of my mother produced the detail that Maury Blair had gravitated from Flint to Fort Wayne, Indiana. Bev called the Fort Wayne operator and asked if there was a listing for a Maury Blair.

"No," the operator replied, "but we have a Maurice Blair."

Bev placed a person-to-person call to the number in Fort Wayne and asked the operator to ask for Maury Blair instead of Maurice. I listened on an extension phone as a man answered.

"Yes, this is Maury Blair."

It was a weird sensation to hear my own voice on the other end of the line. But the match was undeniable.

Bev asked him if he were the Maury Blair who had lived and worked in Flint, Michigan, in 1937 at Irving Machine Parts.

"Yes, I'm that same Maury Blair."

Bev explained that her husband was a minister with the same name who was trying to locate his real father, and that the search had led right to him.

"Are you the right man?" Bev asked eagerly, sure that he was.

There was a moment of silence, then the tense response: "No, I don't think so."

Bev bit her lip. She realized too late that she had told too much too soon, and now she had few options. She cut the conversation short — "All right, thank you" — and hung up.

We held a hurried, nervous conference. We had burst the bubble now. In the drama of encountering my biological father for the first time in any fashion, we were not sure what to do next. Set it all aside and forget it? Pursue him? Try to meet him? And what had we done to the man himself? Was he standing at his phone in Fort Wayne in tears? In fear? Did he expect us to blackmail him? What did his family know about the Alice Wick of so many summers ago?

We decided that I should call him back.

When I introduced myself on the phone, he asked me to wait a moment. I heard him put the phone down, then I heard a door close, then he picked up the phone again. I explained my story to him, gingerly avoiding any suggesting of accusation that would put him on the defensive. This, I figured, could be my last shot. After this conversation, he could change his phone number, move to a different city, alter his identity, or lose me forever by any one of numerous other methods.

But he was too intrigued, as I would have been in his shoes, to let the opportunity pass, and he asked me question after question about my work, my family, my situation in life. He never admitted to fathering me, never made any reference that could be so construed, but his interest in me was fatherly, and intensely so.

At the end of the conversation, we agreed that I would call him again sometime in the future and talk further.

As I hung up, I realized I was breathless.

The one long-distance encounter satisfied me for a long time. Life went on, our work continued, the ministry commanded our attention month after month with few let-ups. But the seed of the unknown had taken root, and the next autumn Bev and I were driving home from a conference in Missouri when we decided to stop in Fort Wayne.

A phone book in a public phone booth told us the address of Maurice Blair. Nervously we drove by the place and — grasping at the moment for posterity — took pictures of the house. At the nearest corner we parked the car and prayed that he would walk out the front door so I could just see him, without the trauma of knocking on his door.

But impulse seized me as I waited. I jumped out of the car and walked to the door and rang the bell. If anyone else came to the door, I would ask for directions to some imaginary address.

I read the name on the door: Maurice D. Blair.

When he swung the door open, I had the odd sensation all over again of meeting myself — except that here, now, it was face to face, with all the complicated nuances of the visual. He was some thirty, perhaps thirty-five years older than I, taller, broader, and yet in all other respects virtually identical to me. The effect was so startling that we were both stunned, unable to speak or move for an endless moment. Here gazed the child of woe into his father's eyes, and the accidental father in the face of his unknown son. I was more a part of him than he was of the woman he had slept with to conceive me, and yet we had never met, never touched. He had left me behind, unwittingly, in my mother's womb. Now, in this moment of rare truth, the wild oat had come back to haunt its sower.

As I stood transfixed, I heard voices in the background of the house. I knew better than to introduce myself by name. But he didn't know that yet. I could read his mind as I watched his eyes; he knew I could ruin him with a word, a phrase, in a matter of seconds. Behind those eyes so like my own, he was masking the terror of exposure.

I ached to tell him who I was, to resolve the question that would linger forever if I didn't: were we truly father and son? I knew by all logic there could be no other explanation for the multitude of coincidence that converged our lives at this point. But still, to sit and talk with him, to explore, to fill in the innumerable gaps, would have somehow completed my earthly self.

Instead, as I saw the fear on his face, I mumbled a request for directions to some fabricated address. The question was probably incoherent, but little matter. He mumbled in reply that he could not help me, and that was probably true in several different ways.

I told him I would try further down the street, and I turned to walk toward the car. I did not turn around, but Bev viewed everything from the parking place. She saw the man step out onto the veranda and watch us until we were out of sight.

The rest of the drive to Canada was accomplished in silence. I was numb. There was no way to take the kind of event it had been and put it immediately into sentences and paragraphs of conversation. After thirty-five years on this earth, I had confronted the man who had given me life, and for the moment the encounter had drawn the life out of me.

I did not have the heart to pursue him. Each time over the space of the following months that I came to the point of picking up the telephone, I could only see his terrified face, looking perhaps like a grown-up version of my own face in the days of facing Cyrus.

So it was a full year before I finally placed the call. It was a cordial talk, a short conversation in which I suggested that we have coffee together sometime when I was in Fort Wayne. He agreed pleasantly, and we hung up. I did not mention the incident at the door. I thought we could talk about that in person.

We never talked again. In the next year he died of a heart attack.

Later I tracked down Maurice D. Blair's younger brother and discovered through him that I had half-brothers and half-sisters living in Fort Wayne. But for me, the quest was largely over. Only for the record books, only for the satisfaction of human fancy and inquisitiveness, had I searched out my father at all. Completeness for me never hinged on discovering the source of my genetics. Completeness for me had occurred in that squalid little house in Paris, Ontario, years before, as I thumbed the pages of a borrowed book in my lonely upstairs bedroom. Completeness for me had come in that moment, as I met the Father who had been watching me and loving me all along.

God had never been confused about my bloodline. "Before I formed thee in the belly," He declared through Jeremiah 1:5, "I knew thee; and before thou camest forth out of the womb I sanctified thee." My earthly bloodline never restricted Him. I was His. He would provide a new bloodline anyway. In those marvelous moments as He revealed Himself to me, I became the person I was destined to be, scandalous heritage notwithstanding. Once the child of woe, I became instantaneously a child of the King.

The agonies of my youth remained vivid in my memory, although my Father healed the pain. The victimization of the innocent, like the suffering of the saints, can never be fully explained in this life. Even godly Job may have only suffered his personal horror for the benefit of those of us who could read his account and learn from it centuries later.

I was fortunate. God gave me a work in which I could trade my own troubled past for the help of others later on. In my ministry, I have been privileged to work with hundreds and hundreds of people who needed the counsel of a person who had been there, a person who had faced his own Cyrus Wick. God has given me the opportunity to speak at youth camps, Christian businessmen's conventions, rock festivals, even overseas. Most recently I have been able to establish a nationwide evangelism ministry called Break-Through, which includes counseling for troubled youth, a 24-hour help-line, street witnessing, kids' clubs, radio outreach, and a Break-Through Band. In these satisfying ways and more, the Heavenly Father has redeemed the lost years for me many times over by giving me the opportunity of declaring the phenomenon of His loving power: If He could rescue me from that hopelessness, He can rescue anybody from anything.

A PERSONAL MESSAGE FROM MAURY

God was not out of control, nor wringing His hands in despair as I grew up in the old man's angry shadow. He was not frustrated, nor struggling to pull events into order. He is the sovereign, and just as I was in His keeping, destined for my personal transformation, you are in His keeping at this moment. Just as the Father waited for me to enter into His love, He is waiting for you.

Many fail to enter in because they feel inadequate. But I found the Father to require no adequacy. I had none. The children that God adopts are often misfits, as I was. But we misfits are the children needing love the most, and needing to express it. Perhaps that's why God loves you and me so much.

Give the Father your love. Enter in. As you do, you will discover as I did that He has indeed called you and sanctified you for a special place in His Kingdom.

You are not a lost and forsaken child wandering without hope through a mindless universe. Your place at the Father's banquet table was set for you before your birth. Your special place in His heart was established before you could ever love Him back. It was not a place you won by your goodness. It was a place God set for you because He loves you — the person you are.

When you step into that love, when you take your place at the table, your destiny unfolds — your identity is finally complete.

When you accept Jesus Christ as your Saviour, you finally make contact with the love of your Heavenly Father. When you let Him put your sins and shortcomings behind you, the future truly begins.

He knows your name, and He is whispering it, as He waits for you to answer.

Maury Blair

For Booking Information:
MAURY BLAIR
Breakthrough Youth Ministries
650 Broadview Avenue
Toronto, Ontario
M4K 2P1
Canada
(416) 463-4235